T0128474

READY ...
SET ...
GOD

A Football Story with Illustrations
that Share Evidence for Christianity

JASON M. JOLIN

WESTBOW
PRESS®
A DIVISION OF THOMAS NELSON
& ZONDERVAN

WestBow Press books may be ordered through booksellers or by contacting:

WestBow Press
A Division of Thomas Nelson & Zondervan
1663 Liberty Drive
Bloomington, IN 47403
www.westbowpress.com
1 (866) 928-1240

ISBN: 978-1-9736-4589-4 (sc)
ISBN: 978-1-9736-4588-7 (hc)
ISBN: 978-1-9736-4590-0 (e)

Library of Congress Control Number: 2018913727

Print information available on the last page.

WestBow Press rev. date: 12/31/2018

Contents

Acknowledgments

I want to thank those who read my book and provided feedback, encouragement, and support. These include my amazing wife, Kristina Jolin, whom I am so fortunate to have as my love and companion and truly appreciate the support she has provided to me and this book; my fantastic parents, Dennis and Deborah Jolin, who have always been there for me; my wonderful parents-in-law, Marcel and Lorraine Laplante, who have always treated me like a real member of the family; my friend Dr. Mark Jordi, a Christian trained in science, whom I respect and trust; and my pastor of twenty-five years, the Reverend Robert Howard ("Pastor Bob"), who has been a great spiritual shepherd.

Most of all, I want to thank my Lord and Savior, Jesus Christ, for sacrificing Himself to provide a path of salvation for mankind and enabling me to work in the discipline of Christian apologetics.

This book is dedicated to my children—Trevor, Toriana, and Titus—whom I love and am proud of. I hope it is beneficial to them and anyone else who may benefit from my two passions, football and apologetics.

Introduction

What is the most important decision you will make in your entire life? There are many important decisions we make along the journey of life, but I'm asking about the absolute, most important one. What would you say?

In less than thirty seconds, you can probably name a few possibilities. Whom will I marry? Where will I live? Should I have kids? What will I do for work? Obviously, these types of questions come to mind because they have such a huge impact on your life. If you change the decision, your journey and destination will be quite different.

Yet as important as any of those decisions are (or were), they aren't *the* most important one. I am talking about a decision that will impact you forever. Literally forever. A decision that will determine the eternal destination of your soul. Don't brush over the word *eternity*; it is essential. We tend to live for the here and now, but at some point, we will move beyond this life to a final destination.

You may be thinking, *I'm all set. I already have my beliefs about God and life after death.* Maybe you are a Christian or follow a different religion. Perhaps you contend that God doesn't exist ("atheist"), or maybe you would say you don't know ("agnostic"). You may already have an opinion about heaven and how to get there. How did you arrive at these conclusions? Are you open to some important evidence that may inform your position?

Let me be very clear: *This book isn't intended to be disrespectful or insulting.* I respect everyone's free will to choose what he or she believes, but I feel compelled to share critical information most people are unaware of. Whatever your current view is, it will take time to consider the information in this book and perhaps incorporate it into your spiritual journey. Thank you for taking this time to read and reflect.

According to Christianity, everyone makes a decision about God, which leads to one of two paths—either to a place of extraordinary happiness (heaven) or to a place of horrible torment (hell). If this is true, it's easy to see that *the most important decision you will ever make is about God, since it will determine where you spend eternity.* How can anything in this life compare to eternity? One is like the blink of an eye compared to the other.

Don't get me wrong. Life is very important. But let's put it in perspective. If you could live your perfect life, what would it look like? President of the United States? CEO of your company? Super Bowl-winning quarterback? Oscar-winning actor? Winner of the lottery and traveler of the world? Beautiful spouse, two kids, and a great home with a white picket fence? Imagine you were actually able to live your dream life. Then what? Your life may be fantastic, but it's only a nanosecond compared to eternity. I want to enjoy life and make a difference in the world, but I also have an interest in what happens when I die. This isn't "dwelling on death" but rather being mindful of what is at stake.

This book is about considering your eternal destination.

My Two Passions

I started writing this book on the same day I received news that my grandfather (Orville Roberts) had passed away. His death wasn't unexpected. He was ninety-four and battling a staph infection that had gotten into his bloodstream. It eventually shut down his organs, and he slowly faded away. I remember him for his kindness and generosity. Sometimes death wakes us up from the busyness of life to remind us that we are mortal and will someday face a similar fate. Morbid? Maybe. But truthful. This book is about hope for life after death (more on that later).

In some way it seems fitting to begin this book today since one of my earliest memories as a child was at my grandparents' house in Milwaukee, Wisconsin. I was probably three or four years old, but I faintly recall my dad and grandfather yelling at the TV set. "Go! Go! Go!" When I looked at what they were yelling at, I saw a football player running down the sideline for a touchdown. I don't know whether that was *the* trigger, but it is my earliest memory about football. Whether it was watching football on TV, playing a pickup game with friends, or designing my own set of football plays, I have loved the sport my whole life—addicted some might say but an avid fan nonetheless.

Decades later, I developed a new passion—evidence for God. I read a book called *More Than a Carpenter* by Josh McDowell that provided reasons to believe Christianity was true. Very interesting. Later I read another book, *I Don't Have Enough Faith to Be an Atheist* by Norman Geisler and Frank Turek. Wow! I was blown away. It provided a comprehensive case for Christianity.

I was captivated by the topic of Christian apologetics, which is a rational defense of the Christian faith using evidence from disciplines such as philosophy, science, and history.

I spent the next several years devouring books on this topic. I eventually went to Biola University and earned a master's degree in Christian apologetics. I enjoy evidence, logic, and debates as well as teaching—and believe the truth about God is essential. I considered myself a Christian before, but now I was convinced with my mind.

Purpose of This Book

So what is this book about? Football? God? Life after death? Yes, yes, and yes. Essentially, it is about giving you information regarding the most important decision of your life. *What is the truth about God and my commitment to it?* The decision actually has two parts: looking beyond our preferences to discover the truth about God.

Then it becomes personal—our decision about whether to truly commit to that truth.

Is there anything more important than getting eternity right? No reasonable person can dismiss it. That said, most people aren't aware of the evidence. Being sincere isn't enough; we must be committed to what is the actual truth about God.

There are already numerous great books on apologetics, but to appeal to a different audience, I have decided to combine Christian apologetics with a football story. I will be using elements from the game of football to illustrate some key evidence. Each chapter will be fairly brief, but it will always include two parts:

1. The first part of each chapter will be a fictional football story, written from a first-person perspective. It is one continuous story that begins in chapter 1 and continues through chapter 13. This first part will end with the following symbol:

2. The second part of each chapter will explain how an aspect of football from that chapter illustrates a key piece of evidence for Christianity. This part is organized by questions. Feel free to read or skim questions that are of interest.

It's important to note that number one is a fictional story, but number two is nonfiction, providing real evidence and rationale.

I hope the illustrations are helpful, but I want to be very clear that no analogy or illustration is 100 percent perfect. Illustrations are meant to be helpful to understand and remember a key concept, but there will always be some differences and a point at which the analogy doesn't fit. Moreover, *there is no substitute for reading the Bible and getting the truth about God directly from His Word.* That said, I hope this book provides some interesting and helpful illustrations.

Is this book for Christians or non-Christians? Both. See below.

Christians

If you are a Christian, my hope is that this information will strengthen your love for God with your mind. Why is this important? Consider Jesus's response when asked what is the most important command. "Jesus replied: 'Love the Lord your God with all your heart and with all your soul and with all your mind'" (Matthew 22:37 NIV).

As Christians, we are called to love God with our whole being, including our minds. This emphasis is sorely lacking in the church today. In fact, it's why some people are walking away from their faith. This should *not* be the case; the evidence is compelling.

Another reason this book may be helpful to Christians is because the Bible says *Christians should be ready to provide an answer to anyone who asks about their faith.* "But in your hearts revere Christ as Lord. Always be prepared to give an answer to everyone who asks you to give the reason for the hope that you have. But do this with gentleness and respect" (1 Peter 3:15 NIV). (The word "answer" in this verse is from the Greek word "apologia", which is where we get the word apologetics).

All Christians should be ready to share what they believe and why. The why will likely include a personal testimony about what God has done for them; however, this may not be enough. We live in a skeptical society, where some people may desire or need some evidence. Consequently, all Christians should have at least some of the basics on Christian apologetics. It's worth noting that the end of the verse above states that our approach needs to be done with gentleness and respect, not arrogance or disrespect.

What if you claim to be a Christian but aren't truly following the Lord? This situation could be extremely dangerous—a false sense of security. Jesus warns that there will be some people who claim to be Christians but won't enter heaven. "Not everyone who says to me,

'Lord, Lord,' will enter the kingdom of heaven, but only the one who does the will of my Father who is in heaven. Many will say to me on that day, 'Lord, Lord, did we not prophesy in your name and in your name drive out demons and in your name perform many miracles?' Then I will tell them plainly, 'I never knew you. Away from me, you evildoers!'" (Matthew 7:21–23 NIV).

Perhaps the biggest misconception today about Christianity is that being a good person gets you into heaven. This belief isn't Christianity at all. The Bible says we are all sinners facing judgment and that salvation is only by God's grace through the death of Jesus, not by good deeds. "For by grace you are saved through faith, and this is not from yourselves; it is God's gift—not from works, so that no one can boast" (Ephesians 2:8–9 HCSB).

However, our hearts determine whether we are true followers of Jesus. Good deeds are a subsequent response to our commitment. Only you know whether you are truly following Christ or whether you should examine your commitment. Perhaps knowing the evidence for Christianity could strengthen your relationship with God.

Non-Christians

You may be following another religion or reject God entirely. You may be mildly interested or actively seeking. As mentioned above, *my intent isn't to offend or disrespect anyone*; rather, I want to share important information everyone should have in deciding his or her ultimate destiny.

Perhaps your passions and hobbies in life seem more important. You may be apathetic toward the topic of religion. Consider this very important question from Jesus: "What good is it for someone to gain the whole world, yet forfeit their soul?" (Mark 8:36 NIV).

Jesus was stressing what is most important—eternity! There is nothing wrong with living a good life, but it pales in comparison to the truth about knowing God and going to heaven forever.

Although the focus of this book is on evidence, I don't want to miss a very important point—*God's love for you*. You may have seen signs at a football game or other sporting events that display "John 3:16," which is perhaps the most famous verse of the Bible. "For God so loved the world that he gave his one and only Son, that whoever believes in him shall not perish but have eternal life" (John 3:16 NIV).

This verse represents good news, a message of hope and a means for salvation. It is also an expression of how much God loves us. He loves you! He loves you more than you understand. No matter what your situation is, God wants you. You are His child. But if your mind is blocking your heart from pursuing God, I hope the information in this book will help break down some of those barriers.

Getting Started

The title of this book is a play on words. In football, a quarterback initiates a play by saying something similar to, "Ready. Set. Go." In this book, "Ready ... Set ... God" represents a spiritual journey. It can be your journey.

- **Ready**—Are you ready? Are you open to searching for the truth about God? If necessary, are you truly open to the possibility of changing your mind? This is an important first step. We must be honest with ourselves. We all have preconceived opinions about religion, but hopefully the magnitude of what is at stake will help us to be open minded. No one walks into a doctor's office with his or her mind made up about treatment for a serious illness. The person is willing to listen with an open mind.
- **Set**—This step, SET, is about **S**earching the **E**vidence for **T**ruth. It is the main point of the book. Although this isn't

a comprehensive source on Christian apologetics, it will provide some key evidence.

- **God**—This is about making a decision to follow the truth about God. It isn't enough to simply know the truth. We must commit to it. More on that later.

I hope this book is helpful with the most important decision of your life—choosing your eternal destination.

Let's start with some football.

1

The Beginning

My name is Adam. I want to tell you about the most important day of my life—a football game I have spent years preparing for. It is the pinnacle of a long journey I can summarize in one word—*sacrifice*. Countless hours of practice. Multiple injuries. Literally, blood, sweat, and tears. I had played in a lot of games, but this one means the most by far. Everything comes down to one specific moment, but let's start from the beginning.

The stadium is trembling like a small earthquake. I look down at my cleats, which are shaking, and feel the vibrations in my calf muscles. I am standing on the sideline, helmet cradled in my arm. With the game about to begin, I take a moment to soak in the scene.

Although it is still daytime, the stadium lights are already on, anticipating the sun's descent. The sky is clear. The air is fresh and crisp; it's not too cold yet. The weather is perfect right now, but soon the temperatures are expected to drop below freezing, and some snow is on the way. Thousands of people are on their feet, most in a state of frenzy. The place is electric, and noise level almost deafening—not a surprise with a championship at stake.

But for me, this game has additional meaning. It is the first time I am playing against my brother, Chad. To say we have a strained relationship would be an understatement. At one point we were close—very close. But after Mom passed away, we went in different directions. He is Mr. Perfect. Hard worker, friendly to everyone, always positive. And he never seems to do anything wrong. Wish I could say the same. I struggled in school, fought with my dad, and even got in trouble with the law.

Mom's death impacted me severely. We were very close, and her death was unexpected. She died suddenly of a heart attack. Sure, my father and brother were deeply impacted; but for me, her death turned my world upside down. Everything changed, and I struggled to function. My family tried to be there for me, but it wasn't until I found football that I had something to channel my emotions. My emptiness. My anger. Coach Stan, my current coach, encouraged me to devote myself fully to the game, and it would solve my problems. Football has allowed me to find (or lose) myself.

I am now the quarterback of one of the best teams. I love my teammates and coaches, whom I consider family. They are closer to me than blood. I still feel a tug in my heart toward my father and brother, but years of brokenness have created a barrier, a divide I don't know how to bridge. A part of me feels, or hopes, that if I win this game, it may somehow resolve family tension and reconcile unspoken issues. I want to make my dad proud of me. I want to beat my older brother for once in my life.

Ironically, Chad is the star quarterback on the other team. He is, without question, the best player. *I really want to beat him. I have never wanted anything more in my life.*

A slap on my shoulder pad from a teammate awakens me from my thoughts. I flash a grin and a nod. I let the painful thoughts of family begin to fade. Then I force them out completely—burying them with anger. *Focus!* I tell myself, reminding myself of what is at stake.

I turn my attention to the field. Both teams are lined up for the kickoff, ready to begin the game. The crowd has reached its highest decibel level, uncomfortable to the ears.

A player from Chad's team, clearly the smallest on the field, lifts his right arm, signaling he is about to start. His name is Ian. Thousands of eyes are on him. He looks right and left, checking the readiness of his teammates. He turns his attention to the target, a football sitting on an orange tee, pointing upright.

My gaze centers on the football as well. It is sitting there innocently, waiting to get blasted. It is bent at a slight angle to allow the kicker to get underneath it with his kick. *It all starts there,* I think. *This entire battle, which both teams have spent months preparing for, begins when that leather object is kicked.*

Ian eases forward slowly, taking a few steps toward the ball and gaining speed as he closes in on the target. He plants his left foot next to the ball. With a huge windup, he swings his right leg sharply, smacking the ball about sixty yards across the stadium.

The game has begun.

How Does the Beginning of a Football Game Relate to Evidence for God?

The kickoff that starts a football game illustrates one of the most powerful arguments for the existence of God. *Everything that has a beginning must have a cause,* whether it's the start of a football game or the entire universe.

Imagine an empty football stadium. No players. No coaches. No fans in their seats. Nothing but silence. A football is set up on a tee in the field, but no one is in sight. Does the ball ever get kicked? Does the game ever get started? Of course not. You need a person who makes a decision to kick the ball and then actually does so. Without that kick, the game never begins.

This is simple cause and effect, a principle everyone understands. It is also foundational to science. No one believes things happen (effects) without a cause. If you saw a new dent in your car, you would wonder what caused it.

The same principle of cause and effect applies to the universe. We know the universe had a beginning. There was literally no time, space, or matter until the universe came into existence.[1] Did it all pop into existence by itself (uncaused), or is it more reasonable that something (or someone) caused it? Since everything we see in the world today functions under cause and effect, why wouldn't the origin of the universe also need a cause?

A kickoff helps illustrate this concept, but the cause of the universe is far more extraordinary. At least with the game of football, the ball and field already exist prior to the kick,[2] but the universe was literally created from nothing (*creation ex nihilo*), an idea that is consistent with the Bible. This illustration of cause and effect applies to other sports. Someone makes the first pitch (baseball), drops the puck (hockey), tosses the ball for the tip-off (basketball), and so forth. Since both the football game and the universe had a beginning, someone or something must have caused them.

How Do We Know the Universe Had a Beginning?

Virtually everyone today, including scientists, believes the universe had a beginning. But this wasn't always the case. Prior to the twentieth century, atheists contended that the universe was eternal. Recent scientific evidence confirms what the Bible claimed centuries ago—that the universe had a beginning. Although almost no one questions this fact, two points of evidence I like are provided below—one from philosophy and one from science (feel free to skip this answer if this question isn't of interest).

I.   **Philosophy:** Prior to the scientific evidence discovered over the past one hundred years, certain philosophers argued that the concept of time supported the universe having a beginning. Below is one approach.
    A.   **Time:** If the universe were infinite, how could you arrive at today? An infinite number of days would have had to pass to get to today, but that isn't possible. It would be like waiting for a train to arrive at your station today that first has to make an infinite number of stops before yours. Clearly, the train would never get to you. Infinity

is a concept in mathematics, but it's not practical in reality. It's impossible for an infinite number of events to have occurred.[3] Consequently, it makes more sense that the universe and time itself had a beginning.

II. **Science**: The scientific evidence that the universe had a beginning is very strong, but let me offer one point that I find particularly compelling.

 A. **Energy**: The universe is running out of usable energy.[4] This is based on the second law of thermodynamics, a fundamental law in science. It supports the point that in a closed system where energy cannot be added, the system will tend toward disorder and run out of usable energy. If atheism is true, our universe is a closed system, nothing beyond it. But that means that if the universe were infinite, it would have already run out of usable energy, which is called a "heat death." Since that isn't the case, the universe cannot be infinite—it must have had a beginning.

Why Is God the Best Explanation for the Cause of the Universe?

Since the universe consists of time, space, and matter, whatever caused them to come into existence doesn't have these attributes; in other words, since time, space, and matter came into existence with the universe, the cause of the universe is timeless, spaceless, and immaterial.[5]

Also, the creation of time, space, and matter from nothing indicates that the cause is powerful.[6] We can barely comprehend this extraordinary event. It is literally a miracle to create something from nothing. Naturalism (atheism) cannot account for the cause of the universe since this belief system contends that only nature exists; but the beginning of the universe confirms there was a time when space, time, and matter didn't exist. Consequently, something beyond nature (transcends the universe) must exist.

Finally, the cause of the universe is very likely personal. Why? The act of creating involves a *decision*. How else does something that has always existed (in other words, infinite) move to create a finite universe? It involves a decision to create. Only personal agents with minds make decisions.[7]

Just as nature cannot start a football game (for example, wind blowing the football off the tee), nature doesn't provide an adequate explanation for the beginning of the universe. This is because space, matter, and time didn't exist prior to the beginning; and, it's reasonable to believe that this cause required a decision to create.

In summary, the cause of the universe has these attributes: timeless, spaceless, immaterial, powerful, and personal (we'll add *intelligent* when we discuss design in chapter 2).[8] Doesn't this sound like God? A divine being is the best explanation for the cause of the universe. This conclusion is not based on what we don't know but rather on what *we do know.*

What Is a Logical Summary of This Argument?[9]

1. If the universe had a beginning, something beyond the universe must have caused it.
2. The evidence is compelling that the universe had a beginning.
3. Therefore, something beyond the universe must have caused it.
4. Since the cause is timeless, spaceless, immaterial, and arguably powerful and personal, God is clearly the best explanation.

Skeptic: Who Created God?

Some skeptics ask this question as if it is a gotcha response. In other words, if a Christian cannot answer this question, then the atheist doesn't need to provide an answer regarding the cause of the universe. But this question is irrational for two reasons.

First, it misunderstands the argument. The principle of cause and effect doesn't say *everything* needs a cause, rather only things that had a *beginning*. God, by definition, doesn't have a beginning. God is the uncaused Creator. He's eternal. Therefore, to ask, "Who created God?" is nonsensical. If God had a cause, you would have to ask, "What caused God?"; this questioning would go on infinitely, which obviously doesn't make sense. Something must have always existed.

Second, we know the universe had a beginning, so this response does nothing to explain what caused the universe. It simply tries to avoid the conclusion that is pointing to God.

Is There a Verse in the Bible Related to the Origin-of-the-Universe Argument?

Consider the first verse of the Bible. "In the beginning God created the heavens and the earth" (Genesis 1:1 HCSB).

From this verse, God is cited as the cause of the universe. Scientific discoveries in the twentieth century confirmed that the universe had a beginning—which aligns with God's Word, written thousands of years before this evidence.

Summary Point: Since the universe had a beginning, something that transcends the universe must have caused it, and only God fits this description (timeless, spaceless, immaterial, powerful, and personal).

The next time you see a kickoff to start a football game, perhaps it will remind you that the universe must have had a cause as well—God.

2
Design

Score:

> Chad's team: 0
> Adam's team: 0

Time remaining:

> First quarter, sixty minutes left in the game

As soon as the kickoff takes place, all the anticipation that has been building for hours is released. It's as if the stadium collectively exhales. The battle has begun.

The roar of the crowd fades quickly as fans follow the ball in the air with eager anticipation. The kick is short but very high.

I look downfield at my teammate Evan, who is tracking the ball. He has run to a spot, anticipating its descent, about twenty yards from where I am standing on the sideline. Teammates on the field assemble around Evan, ready to execute their blocking assignments. They hope to provide a running lane and spring a big return.

Evan's arms take position to make the catch, but he makes a terrible mistake. He lowers his head, apparently taking his eyes off the ball to glance at the opposition, which is approaching like a pack of savage wolves. No doubt the sound of clashing football helmets must be intimidating, and the ball seems to be hanging in the air longer than usual.

Evan's head returns upward toward the football, but it's too late. He must have lost track of the ball. It nips his facemask, altering the course from Evan's hands. It goes from bad to worse when the ball hits his left knee and bounces forward toward Chad's team.

My eyes grow wide with disbelief. Butterflies already in my stomach intensify to the point of pain. My thoughts scream, *Get the ball!* Players on the field are literally yelling, "Ball!" and diving for it. The scramble is intense—as if this is the most important object in the world. A pile develops in the middle of the field. Limbs are bending in unnatural and painful positions.

My heart is pounding at a level that is scary. I can actually feel each heartbeat pressing against my football pads. I reach up and put my hand on my chest to try to calm myself. This pounding of my heart reminds me of the medical concerns that almost kept me from playing football. I inherited similar heart problems that took my mother's life, problems that unfortunately run in the family.

When I was a teenager, I had some recurring chest pain, followed by numbness in my left arm. This problem led to months of cardiac testing. I was connected to an EKG machine more times than I can recall. I went through three separate tests that measure a heart's activity during exercise. I think they are part of what is called a "stress test."

The first test was the scariest. After a medical technician injected some dye into my body, he had me run on some type of treadmill. I remember the repetitive thud of my feet against the spinning belt as I worried about how much this one medical test could change my life. It could stop me from playing sports or limit other activities. It could predict a short life span or the need for a heart transplant. I had already lost my mom; I couldn't lose playing football too. Surprisingly the test was done quicker than I expected.

I was afraid to hear the results. I sat in the doctor's office with a large desk in front of me, waiting for his arrival. I heard the doorknob twist and knew it was a matter of minutes before my life was headed one way or the other. He greeted me with a handshake, sat in his chair, and put on a set of glasses. Opening a file, he read me some technical results.

What does it really mean? I wondered. *Get to the point!*

The doctor closed the file and removed his glasses. He looked at me with compassion, knowing what had already happened in our family. I swallowed hard. He said several things, but the one thing, the only thing I heard, was that I was medically cleared to play.

I remember closing my eyes and exhaling a sigh of relief. My head dipped, and my eyelids filled with fluid; I couldn't control my emotions.

Although there were some signs of potential issues with my heart, the evidence wasn't strong enough right now to restrict me from playing. Technically, it was my choice whether to play; but in my mind, there really was no decision. Just in case you're wondering, Chad went through similar testing, but his heart showed absolutely no blemishes. Like I said, Mr. Perfect.

The memories disappear suddenly; I am sucked back to present-day reality. I take a deep breath through my nose to calm myself, opening my mouth to let out a large exhale. I watch the frenzy, hoping for a sign that we have the ball.

Before anyone can get control of the football, it gets smacked away from the pile of bodies. I watch it roll several yards toward me, losing steam as it approaches. It comes to within an inch of the sideline, and I have to resist the temptation to reach down and grab it, an act that would be interference from the sideline. I'm horrified to see someone from Chad's team get to it first. I know him; Michael is his name.

He doesn't just recover the ball; he picks it up and starts running for the end zone. *My* end zone. The action has reignited the crowd. They have jumped to their feet, cheering the runner.

Michael sprints down the sideline. Every step is within inches from touching the white out-of-bounds line. I keep hoping one of his cleats will step on the white line and end this disaster, or maybe someone from my team will push him out. But most of my teammates are still gathered around the original pile.

Someone, get him! I scream in my head.

Michael closes in on the end zone as two players from my team approach him from the side. Michael is within five yards of scoring when they converge. He jumps for the pylon, extending the ball in his right hand. A player from my team simultaneously dives at him, trying to push him out of bounds.

This doesn't stop the inevitable. The ball touches the orange pylon just before both players crash out of bounds.

A referee is standing within a few yards, knees bent and head forward, watching the action intently. He pauses for a moment and then raises both arms.

Touchdown!

Chad's sideline erupts in celebration.

I'm sickened. There is no way the game could have started any worse. I scan the field, hoping to see a yellow handkerchief that might change the outcome. Nothing.

I look up at the replay on the big screen, hoping to see Michael stepping out of bounds before scoring—anything that might trigger a replay challenge. The fresh white paint of the sideline makes it easy to see the results. Each step Michael takes is examined in slow motion. He comes so close to stepping out, but there is a slight thread of green field between his cleats and the white line.

I look at the play one final time. Beneath the rage, a part of me marvels at how Michael tiptoes down the sideline—a perfectly straight line applied with precision. The orange pylon does its job, enabling the refs to confirm the score. The play is extraordinarily close. A football field is designed with precision to enable the game to be played fairly. *It's a game of inches,* I think.

I shake my head in disdain. I was shocked, but now I'm angry. *Time to get revenge.*

A football field is designed with precise order and purpose.

How Does the Design of a Football Field Relate to Evidence for God?

Simply put, design requires intelligence. Anything organized in a complex manner (order) for a specific purpose (or function) comes only from an intelligent being.[10] This is because order and purpose together require intention,[11] which comes only from intelligence.

The earth is filled with things mankind obviously designed and created, such as buildings, cars, planes, televisions, toys, and so forth. Consider the design of a football field. It is a perfect rectangle—100 yards in length and 53.3 yards wide. The sidelines are long, perfectly straight lines—no random curves (this detail alone begins to point toward intelligence). Each end zone is identical, ten yards deep with a yellow goal post in the back, exactly in the middle. Numerous white lines with numbers identify the field position. Could random forces, such as rain, wind, and erosion, produce a football field? Obviously not! Even if you didn't see who designed and built it, the complex organization of the field and stadium, which are created for a specific purpose, clearly points to intelligence.

The same can be said for a football itself. We all know it was designed and manufactured in some factory; but even if we didn't, it clearly has the attributes of design—the perfect oval shape, a line of white stitching, the leather texture with bumps for gripping, and so forth. It's clearly designed for a purpose, which demonstrates intention, and this requires intelligence.

How does this topic relate to God? The universe and planet earth are filled with examples in nature that exhibit design. Some examples include the physical structure of living organisms (for example, the nervous system, circulatory system, digestive system, and so forth), the ability of atoms to connect to form molecules (chemistry), the movement of planets around the sun (physics), and so forth. There are millions of examples in nature of complex structures and processes operating with a specific purpose. The question is whether what appears to be designed could have occurred by chance. Atheists will say yes, while those who believe in God (theists) say a divine architect (a.k.a. God) is the best explanation.

How do we determine who is right? There are some examples of design in nature that are so powerful that chance isn't a realistic option. One of the most powerful arguments for design is the origin of life. How does nonliving matter become a living organism? How could the building blocks necessary for life assemble naturally and become a viable living organism? They can't. Even the simplest life is so incredibly complex that it's mathematically impossible to have occurred by chance.[12]

Another example is the extraordinary design in the universe that allows for life to exist. Let's look closer at this powerful design argument that has gotten recent notoriety, especially in the scientific community—the fine-tuning of the universe.

What Is This Idea about Fine-Tuning in the Universe?

Could a football game be played on a smaller field? Yes. Could it be played without white lines and numbers? Sure. It may be a little more difficult to play, but it can be done. However, there are limits. What if the sidelines had sharp curves instead of straight lines? What if part of the field was in a swamp or if there was a steep hill? Would it be fair if one end zone were two times bigger than the other? In these various scenarios, the football game would be unfair, if not impossible. In other words, a field is designed to play the game fairly.

The parameters in the universe and earth that allow for life to exist are far, far more precise. Changing one parameter, even slightly, could have a detrimental effect to the point that a recognizable universe may not exist or be able to support life. These parameters imply design. Let's discuss this concept in more detail.

The universe has certain laws of nature that are necessary for things to exist, including gravity, strong nuclear force, electromagnetic force, and so forth. What produced these laws of nature that govern the universe? Chance? Or a powerful and intelligent Creator?

In addition to the very existence of these laws, they must have extraordinarily precise values; even the slightest difference could have a serious impact on the universe and parameters required to support life. In other words, you need the law of nature and a very specific value.[13] What caused both to come into existence with the universe? A divine Creator makes the most sense.

What Are Some Attributes of the Universe and Earth That Clearly Point to Them Being Designed?

There are several important attributes in the universe. Below are just four examples, the fundamental forces in nature:

- **Strong nuclear force**: This force in nature holds protons and neutrons together within atoms. If it were 4 percent stronger, diprotons, which is an atom with two protons and no neutrons, would form and cause stars to use up their nuclear fuel; but if it were 10 percent weaker, carbon, oxygen, and nitrogen would be unstable.[14] In either scenario, physical life wouldn't be possible.[15]
- **Electromagnetic force**: This force holds electrons in their orbitals in an atom. If the force were stronger or weaker, we wouldn't have adequate chemical bonding,[16] which enables the various elements in the universe.
- **Weak nuclear force**: This force controls the radioactive decay rate, and the strength of this force is in just the right balance to allow for light and heavy elements.[17] If the force were altered by 1 part in 10^{100}, the universe wouldn't be life permitting.[18]
- **Gravity**: This force draws together objects that have mass. It keeps us from flying into space. It enables planets in the solar system to maintain their orbits around the sun. Altering this force, even very slightly (1 part in 10^{60}), would prohibit life in the universe.[19]

Separately, Earth has a number of conditions that are just right for the planet to support life. If any of these parameters varied even slightly, life couldn't exist. What are some obvious examples?

- **Distance from the sun**: Earth is the right distance from sun to provide the necessary amount of heat. If it were closer, we would burn up; if it were farther away, we would freeze.
- **Rotation speed**: Earth rotates in twenty-four-hour periods. If it were slower, temperature changes would be too dramatic for life to exist; and, if faster, wind speeds would be detrimental.[20]

Isn't It Possible That All the Parameters of the Universe and Earth Happened by Chance?

Based on current estimates, it's mathematically impossible for these parameters to have occurred by chance. According to astrophysicist Dr. Hugh Ross, the universe and earth have numerous attributes to support life. Specifically, the universe has more than 100 attributes,[21] and Earth has almost 400 attributes[22] (these numbers are obviously subject to change with new discoveries).

Dr. Ross calculates the chances of any planet having all the attributes required to support life at 1 chance in 10^{556}.[23] That is equivalent to 1 chance in 10, followed by another 555 zeros! The vast number of planets in the universe, estimated at 10^{22},[24] isn't nearly enough to overcome the extraordinary fine-tuning required to support life. The probability (or improbability) of having a planet support life, without divine intervention, is beyond comprehension.

The bottom line is that even if the estimates are off a little or if new discoveries alter the calculations, chance is still mathematically impossible. The best explanation is that the parameters of the universe and earth are intentionally designed, a conclusion that implies an intelligent Creator. Again, this reasoning is not based on what we don't know but rather on what *we do know*.

What Is a Logical Summary of This Argument?

1. The universe and earth are finely tuned for life to exist.
2. The fine-tuning is due either to random chance or to intentionally being designed by a divine architect (God).
3. It is mathematically impossible for the fine-tuning to have occurred by chance.
4. Therefore, God is the best explanation.

Skeptic: Maybe There Are an Infinite Number of Universes and Our Universe Happens to Be the Right One for Life

What is the primary response by scientists who don't believe God designed the universe? It is called the "multiverse theory," which suggests there are an infinite number of universes that exist, and our universe just happens to have all the right parameters to allow life to exist. In other words, the chance of one universe having all these attributes is statistically impossible, so there must be an infinite number of them to explain why it's conceivable that our universe is "just right."

What's wrong with this theory? There is no evidence; it is completely theoretical. Since these other alleged universes exist outside our universe, there is no way to verify them. How is that science? It's not. It's a position for people who don't want to admit that God is the best explanation for the evidence. They are searching for and adhering to natural explanations (naturalism or atheism) even if the explanations lack evidence or are opposed to the evidence.

Is There a Verse in the Bible That Relates to the Design Argument?

Consider the following verse from the book of Romans, which the apostle Paul wrote: "For since the creation of the world God's invisible qualities—his eternal power and divine nature—have been

Jason M. Jolin

clearly seen, being understood from what has been made, so that people are without excuse" (Romans 1:20 NIV).

According to this verse, God's existence is obvious based on apparent design in nature.

Summary Point: God is the best explanation for the extraordinary design of the universe and earth to allow for life to exist.

The next time you notice the design of a football or a football field, perhaps it will remind you that an intelligent Creator, God, clearly designed the universe, Earth, and other things in nature.

3
Morality

Score:

Chad's team: 10 (Chad's team just added a field goal to increase their lead.)

Adam's team: 0

Time remaining:

First quarter, fifty-one minutes left in the game

The game has progressed a little further, and things have only gotten worse. It's still early, but we are down ten points in less than ten minutes. The score has shaken our confidence and left my team a bit stunned.

So far, our offense has done nothing. Their defense has been aggressive. They seem faster, stronger, and one step ahead of us on every play. Making matters worse, we just lost our fastest receiver, Joe, to an injury. Everything seems to be going against us. We need to get a first down on this next play, or we give the ball back to Chad's team, who may score again.

The play call comes in from the sideline. I lean into the huddle and scan the eyes of my teammates. I don't like the looks on their faces. Tension. Fear. Doubt. Without anyone saying it, we all realize that if the deficit gets larger, the hole may be too large to climb out.

But right now I'm less concerned about the score and more worried about playing while tight and nervous. That's a recipe for disaster. How do I motivate my teammates? What do I say?

I bark instructions for the play but pause before breaking the huddle. My eyebrows crumple and nostrils flare, showing some intensity on my face. "Don't let the score get in your head. Don't play with fear! If we doubt ourselves, we've already lost."

I pause to catch my breath and make sure I have everyone's attention.

"Play the game so that, no matter what happens, you will never look back with regret! Let's fight. One play at a time. *One play at a time!*"

I wonder whether my words do anything, but something needed to be said; and as the quarterback, everyone was looking to me.

I don't wait for a reaction. We clap our hands in unison and break the huddle. Everyone jogs to his position. I settle in at the shotgun position and scan the defense, looking for clues that may give away their scheme. I feel the pressure of the moment and take a deep breath to calm myself. As I exhale, I see white air emerge and realize how cold it has become. The sun has set, and the temperature has dropped considerably. Small particles of snow drift in the air.

The noise of the crowd has picked up; spectators have recognized the magnitude of the play at hand. I see a linebacker creeping toward the line, perhaps giving away his intentions. I yell some instructions to the offensive line, pointing out the potential blitzer. The play clock is winding down. Five. Four. Three. Two.

"Go, go, go," I bark. On the third *go*, the ball snaps into my outstretched hands.

I was right about the defense. That linebacker is crashing up the middle and sending the center backpedaling toward me. Instinctively I extend my left hand to stop the momentum. Fortunately, another offensive lineman has slid over to assist the center, stopping the penetration. My pre-snap warning definitely helped. It has bought me another second, but the rest of the offensive line is collapsing. I know I have only another moment before the pressure breaks through and I am buried by the defense.

I scan the field and see my primary target sprinting across the middle. I don't hesitate. My release is quick and with confidence. I let the ball rip from my hand just as several bodies from both teams slam into me, and everyone falls like dominoes.

I lose sight of the pass but can tell from the commotion on the field that it connected with its intended target. I'm on the ground but able to move my head to see the rest of the play.

One of my favorite wide receivers has caught the ball. The cornerback covering him attempts to tackle him from behind, but the receiver wrestles away from him, breaking the tackle. The defender is left falling to the ground with a small piece of jersey in hand. My receiver keeps running across the field.

Yes! He's got the first down—and more.

There's no one between him and the end zone; but one defender, Allen, is gaining ground from behind.

Another player from my team, Cain, who was farther downfield, is running to assist by providing a block. From the angle he is coming, there is no way Allen can see him approaching; it's a classic blindside hit.

But rather than give Allen a clean block in the shoulder or midsection, Cain attacks his knee. The vicious lunge catches the unsuspecting defender at the absolute worst time. Allen's leg is firmly planted in the grass when Cain's shoulder drives through the knee, snapping it in the *opposite* way the knee is intended to bend. There is a pop everyone close by can hear. Allen collapses in anguish. He doesn't know it yet, but we will later learn that the kneecap is shattered, tibia cracked, and ligaments shredded.

With no other defender in sight, the receiver reaches the end zone and spikes the ball. My sideline erupts in jubilation. It's our first score of the game. But the injury tempers my joy. Though happy we scored, I'm disgusted by the brutal "cheap shot" hit by Cain. It brings back memories and guilt I buried.

When I first started football, I was driven by anger. It fueled my desire to train hard. I ran with anger. I lifted weights with a sense of rage. I went to football practice, encouraging my emotions to burn within. Fury fed every step.

But allowing this anger to fester consumed me. It spread to other areas of life. This was when my father and I started arguing much more. He tried to be there for me, but my disrespect led to verbal confrontations.

It wasn't until one particular practice when I hurt another player that I realized how far I had slipped. I don't even remember the teammate's name, but he was in the perfect place for me to inflict some pain. The play was a reverse, and my unsuspecting prey was looking the other way. He never saw me coming. I ran full steam, lowered my shoulder, and unloaded on his blindside. It was much more than a normal hit. I was taking out my emotional anguish on him. The hit snapped his neck backward and sent him airborne. His mouthpiece sailed in a different direction. It was a crushing hit that kept him off the field for some time.

Fortunately, he wasn't severely hurt, but it was enough to wake me up. For the first time in a long time, guilt overtook my anger. I was surprised by how quickly rage could change to remorse. My coach seemed to like the aggression, which in some way I found peculiar. I promised myself that I would never take my anger out on another person. It's why I am disgusted by the vicious hit Cain just delivered.

Allen is on the ground, writhing in pain. Medical personnel are quickly on the field, trying to react to his condition. He pounds the ground with his right fist. He must know he is badly injured and won't play again in this game.

Since Allen didn't see the play, he is probably not yet aware that it was clearly a "cheap shot". The crowd reacts to the replay on the big screen in the stadium, which shows Cain deliberately attacking his knee. Boos are heard throughout the stadium, which intensify as more and more fans realize what happened.

Cain doesn't seem to mind. He raises both arms and motions his fingers toward himself as a sign that encourages the crowd to rain down boos. He nods, relishing their displeasure and enjoying the role of a villain. I despise his embracing this role, which to me gives our whole team a bad reputation.

But there is no penalty against Cain. Technically, his malice intent didn't violate any *written* rules of the game. Regardless, he clearly violated an *unwritten* rule. You don't deliberately try to hurt another player.

There is a standard of right and wrong that exists beyond the written rules of the game.

How Does Morality in a Football Game Relate to Evidence for God?

Morality, which describes how people *should* behave, can come only from intelligence. This is because moral rules have purpose and intention. They describe how we *ought* to behave, which may differ from the way we *actually* behave. Nature can describe only what is, not what ought to be.[25] The latter is based on intention, and intention requires a mind.

Moreover, since mankind cannot really change what is good versus evil, the source of morality must transcend mankind—God. We will discuss the source of morality further, but let's explain the difference between moral rules and moral values.[26]

In football, there are many written rules. Violating them triggers a penalty, identified by a yellow handkerchief ("flag") and accompanying consequences. Similarly, everyday life has written rules known as "laws." Breaking them also has consequences. For example, driving on the wrong side of the road is dangerous and illegal. Instead of a flag, you may get a ticket and lose some money or worse.

But there are also unwritten moral rules that exist beyond the laws of society or a football rulebook. There is a right and wrong way to treat people, both in life as well as in a football game. To intentionally hurt a person for no reason is wrong, even if it's not a written rule in the football game. Lying and gossip are wrong, even though they aren't illegal. Adultery is wrong, even if it's not a written law.

In the football story, Cain broke an unwritten rule by intentionally hurting another player. There must be a source for these rules, and we will discuss why God is the best explanation.

In addition to moral rules, there are also moral values, which are the value or worth of things in nature (people, animals, plants, and so forth).[27] Moral rules provide the guidelines for our actions, and moral values determine the degree of rightness or wrongness. For example, hurting the innocent is wrong (rule), but there is a difference between stepping on a worm for fun versus harming a dog—and worse yet, hurting a human being (value). All are wrong, but the degree of wrongness varies because each has a different value or worth.

In our football story, Cain intentionally hurt another player. What if Cain had instead slammed his football helmet against a locker, intentionally damaging both pieces of property? Would this also be wrong? Sure. But although both actions are wrong (rule), they don't have the same degree of wrongness because they have different moral values. The fact that Cain's hit was against a person makes it much worse than damage to a piece of property. What explains how things in nature have different moral values? As we will see, God is the best explanation.

Everyone knows morality exists (other than sociopaths). It impacts decisions we make and how we live our lives. The question is, what is the best explanation for the source of moral rules and values? Let's look at each separately.

Why Is God the Best Explanation for Moral Rules?

Do moral rules come from our parents? No. Our parents might help us become aware of the principles of morality, similar to the fact that they may help us learn about math; but morality isn't grounded in our parents. Why not? Quite simply, if a parent were to teach his or her kids to be racists, would that make racism acceptable? No. We would say the parent is wrong, violating a moral principle that exists beyond the parents. You can pick a number of examples instead of racism, but the point is that parents help us become aware of morality, but they don't determine morality.

Do moral rules come from society? Since countries may vary in cultural values and behavior, many people believe this is a good explanation, but it's not. This is clear when we use the same reasoning as that of the parents. If a society or country decided that a particular race or ethnicity was inferior and began committing genocide, we wouldn't say it's simply their opinion. We would say they are wrong. We would say this action is evil. We would say they are violating a moral standard we all know exists. This is what occurred after World War II. The victorious Allies charged certain people from Nazi Germany with crimes against humanity, violating moral rules that superseded the laws of their country.[28]

Let me go further in explaining why society cannot be the source of morality. Slavery was legal in the United States in the 1800s. If society truly gets to make the rules, then there was nothing wrong with slavery back then because it was merely their opinion at that time. But that isn't the way we view history. We don't consider slavery to be acceptable for them; rather, we say they were wrong. They violated a moral standard that *exists independently from their opinion.*

But if each society really determines morality, then someone couldn't say slavery was wrong in the past. In fact, there is no way to have moral progress in society unless the moral standard supersedes society.[29] Since we all believe each society or country can make moral progress, the standard must exist apart from society. Deep down, we all know this to be true.

Can morality be grounded in personality traits from our DNA? Again, this seems contrary to our moral intuition. If people were born with aggressive tendencies and killed someone, we wouldn't accept their action as okay because it is based on their natural bent. It might explain why the action was committed, but it wouldn't make the action acceptable. It would still be wrong.

As you consider these options, it becomes clear that morality doesn't seem to be grounded in mankind. It isn't a subjective opinion. It appears to be objective, independent from mankind. Although we may have feelings about morality, the rules themselves don't come from inside us; rather, the actions themselves are right or wrong, independent of our feelings (which means the rules are outside us).[30]

In the story, Cain's vicious hit, the action intended to injure a player was wrong. It isn't just our feelings inside that make it wrong. Certain actions themselves are wrong; therefore, the source of these moral rules must be outside mankind. Moreover, since these rules are applicable to all mankind a transcendent source is required. Finally, it makes more sense that moral rules are owed to a person of authority who gives us these commands, since moral obligations are owed to persons, not impersonal forces.[31] A person of authority provides a better explanation for our guilt when we break rules.

Based on all these observations about the nature of morality, God is the best explanation for moral rules.

Why Is God the Best Explanation for Moral Values?

If God isn't the Creator, then everything in nature is just a random collection of atoms. Nothing has intrinsic value. There would be no difference in value between a tree, an insect, a cat, or a human being. But clearly this is contrary to our moral intuition. Deep down we know nature has a hierarchy of value, with humans at the top.[32] All people are valuable.

This makes sense from a Christian perspective because people are made in the image of God. "Then God said, 'Let us make mankind in our image, in our likeness, so that they may rule over the fish in the sea and the birds in the sky, over the livestock and all the wild animals, and over all the creatures that move along the ground.' So God created mankind in his own image, in the image of God he created them; male and female he created them" (Genesis 1:26–27 NIV).

Jesus also supported this point, saying that people are more valuable than birds and sheep.

"So don't be afraid; you are worth more than many sparrows" (Matthew 10:31 NIV).

"He said to them, 'If any of you has a sheep and it falls into a pit on the Sabbath, will you not take hold of it and lift it out? How much more valuable is a person than a sheep! Therefore it is lawful to do good on the Sabbath'" (Matthew 12:11–12 NIV).

But if you remove God, you lose the rationale for why people are distinct from everything else in nature.

That doesn't mean atheists will think people are less valuable than other things in nature, but it does mean their worldview cannot account for this truth in reality.[33] Also, Eastern religions may teach that all nature is "one" (everything is part of one divine substance), and this teaching would also struggle to account for a hierarchy of value in nature.[34] Again, this seems contrary to our moral intuition.

The bottom line is that all people are valuable, and the Bible's teaching regarding man being made in the image of God accounts for why this is the case.

What Is a Logical Summary of This Argument?

1. If morality (rules and values) is independent of mankind, then God (a transcendent source) is the best explanation.
2. Morality is independent of mankind (since the rules and values exists regardless of the opinions of people).

3. Therefore, God is the best explanation for morality.

Skeptic: I Don't Need to Believe in God to Be a Good Person

This is a typical response from the atheist; however, it really misses the point. The argument doesn't claim you need God to be *aware* of morality. You don't need to read the Bible to know what is right or wrong, although it's certainly helpful. You can become aware of morality from parents, teachers, and so forth—similar to the way you become aware of math.

Instead, the argument claims you need God as an adequate explanation for the existence of morality. If you remove God, there really is no foundation for objective moral rules and values.

Is There a Verse in the Bible Related to the Moral Argument?

Consider certain verses from the book of Romans, which the apostle Paul wrote. "So, when Gentiles, who do not have the law, instinctively do what the law demands, they are a law to themselves even though they do not have the law. They show that the work of the law is written on their hearts. Their consciences testify in support of this, and their competing thoughts either accuse or excuse them" (Romans 2:14–15 HCSB).

Paul stated that God's laws are written on people's hearts. Even though Gentiles (non-Jews) didn't have Israel's laws, they still knew right and wrong behavior. This is how everyone can know that God exists, because He has placed His moral standard on everyone's heart.

Summary Point: God is the best explanation for the existence of morality, because the standard for moral rules and values exists beyond the opinion of mankind.

The next time you see a football player deliver a "cheap shot", perhaps it will remind you that morality (right and wrong actions and moral values) requires a source that transcends mankind—God.

4

Information

Score:

Chad's team: 10
Adam's team: 7

Time remaining:

First quarter, forty-eight minutes left in the game

I stroll along the sideline by myself, feeling the cold wind blowing across my face. It's far more refreshing with no helmet. But I'm antsy, eager to get back on the field. Ignited by the last score, my team has all the momentum. It has carried over to our defense, which just made two big plays. One was a big hit that caused a fumble, but Chad's team recovered. Even though we are down by three points, it feels like we are winning. I can feel the energy level back with our team.

I settle into a spot and stand with my hands clasped behind my back. I should be throwing passes to stay warm, but I can't take my eyes off the action. Chad breaks the huddle. His team spreads out to formation and our defense mirrors their positions. The crowd is loud and engaged. I see Chad looking over the defense, which is constantly moving around, making it difficult to decipher their intentions.

Chad's demeanor is that of calmness. I have seen that look before on more than one occasion. It's more than calmness. It's confidence. It's a presence about him that indicates he is in control. Even in times of trouble, he never gets rattled. Despite our differences, I have always appreciated this quality about my brother.

There was one time in particular when I was especially grateful for him. I will never forget it. I was a young teenager looking to fill a void. Unfortunately, it wound up with me being with the wrong crowd. Ahab was someone I knew from school. Same age and similar interest in football, but I had stayed clear of him because of his character. He walked around school with arrogance and insulted anyone he thought was weaker than he—a classic bully.

But one day, he invited me to hang out with his friends. Although I really didn't want to, I was glad I wasn't the victim of his insults. I agreed despite a feeling of uneasiness.

We walked about twenty minutes from school to a tough neighborhood. With every step, I grew more uncomfortable. I felt like I was walking into danger, but I continued anyway. My emotional baggage in life was my excuse for advancing.

We proceeded down a dead-end street to the last house on the left. The yellow paint was worn, and the windows were dirty. I had been in poor neighborhoods before, but something felt different.

We headed to the backyard, where there were two other boys; they looked older than me by a couple of years. They flashed a grin when they saw me. One of them motioned my way with his head, asking, "Who's your friend, Ahab?" Ahab didn't respond to the question; instead he asked whether his mother was home. The backyard was not well maintained, to say the least. It was mainly dirt with a few patches of long grass and a sprinkling of trash. I looked down and noticed an empty beer bottle next to my foot. I was so distracted with the rest of the scene that I had almost stepped on it without noticing.

I thought about telling them I had to leave, but that would surely draw a negative reaction, which I was hoping to avoid. One of Ahab's friends handed him a brown bag. The other stared at me as if sizing me up before a heavyweight fight. Ahab's demeanor had changed from friendly to cold. I felt I had walked into a lion's den.

I didn't know whether I was going to get beaten up or asked to do something illegal. I swallowed whatever saliva I could gather in my mouth. Despair was overtaking my feelings of worry. I felt no hope. Something bad was definitely going to happen.

"Adam!" I heard a familiar voice from the driveway. I turned to see Chad walking toward me. "Where have you been? You need to come home now." I had never been so grateful to see my brother in my entire life. He stopped within a foot of me and put his hand on my head as if to say, *You're a foolish brother, but I love you anyway.* Usually I resisted any hint of Chad's affection, but this time I was too grateful for his presence.

I noticed that Chad was staring down the other boys. His eyes were narrow and seemed to burn with anger. The disposition of the other boys was different. Their snide confidence had changed to uneasiness. Oddly no one said a word. Chad's arm reached around my shoulder and pulled me toward the driveway. We were heading home. I remember thinking, *Thank God!*

Ahab and I never spoke again; it was as if the event never happened. That day I really appreciated Chad's commanding presence and his saving me from whatever was about to happen.

Back to football. The play clock is under ten seconds when I see something click with my brother. He starts motioning with his hands and barking orders to his teammates in a quick and urgent manner. He has clearly noticed something and decided to call an audible, changing the play to take advantage of the defense.

Despite the crowd noise, I can faintly hear, "Red 316! Red 316!" coming from Chad's cupped hands around his mouth. Chad claps his hands, and the ball snaps just before the play clock expires. Our defense gets a great jump, an aggressive blitz; six defenders come after him.

Unfortunately, Chad saw the blitz coming and changed the play at the line of scrimmage; his audible is perfect. He quickly finds his target. Abraham is running a quick slant route over the middle of the field, which he runs behind another wide receiver to get wide open. Chad floats a touch pass over an extended hand, hitting him in stride. Right after the throw, a linebacker swallows Chad. But the defense is too late.

The pass is perfect. Abraham catches it without breaking stride. A defender trying to cover him is two steps behind. He dives at Abraham's legs, but he is too far away. His arm hits nothing but air, and his facemask eats a pile of grass.

With most of the defense attacking the quarterback, Abraham has a wide-open field. He is the fastest player on the field, and it shows. A safety on the other side is trying to close the gap, but he slows to a jog when he realizes his attempt is futile. Once Abraham has some daylight, no one can lay a hand on him.

Touchdown! All our momentum is gone.

An audible is a code (information) to change the play.

How Does an Audible Relate to Evidence for God?

Information requires intelligence. Random letters jumbled together, such as "YGLAALOTBMEDOTFAO," are meaningless. But the exact same set of letters organized in a certain way, "FOOTBALL GAME TODAY," produce a meaning beyond the letters themselves. The letters are material symbols, but the message itself is immaterial. Since it has purpose and intention, it can come only from intelligence.

In football, teams have huge playbooks with assignments for their players. Each play has a specific purpose and unique name, such as "Triple-Y-Right-Genesis-12-T-3." Although the name may look random and sound like nonsense, it has a specific meaning the coaches designed to communicate assignments to each player. An audible, which a quarterback calls at the line of scrimmage to change the play, isn't a group of random, meaningless words. It is a coded message for his team. It is information teammates decipher to know their new assignments.

Also, when you see a football play illustrated by Xs and Os, you recognize that an intelligent person designed the patterns of the play with a certain purpose in mind. There is a deeper meaning beyond the letters and arrows. There is intention; and this requires a person of intelligence, not random chance.

How does information in football (design of a play, an audible, and so forth) relate to evidence for God? There is an extraordinary amount of information in nature, which couldn't have come randomly from natural forces. DNA contains information inside the cells of living things that controls the development of an organism as well as other activities. How do the cells of your body know how to function in a certain way, such as growth and healing? The information contained in DNA provides instructions for activities in our physical bodies; it is best explained by a divine Creator.

Why Is God the Best Explanation for Information in Nature?

A divine intelligence (God) is the best explanation for two reasons.

First, the *nature of information requires intelligence.* The message itself is immaterial, separate from the letters themselves. The meaning isn't something that can be touched or seen; rather it is interpreted by a mind. Since the message has intent and purpose, it requires a sender.[35] If you find a piece of paper in the woods with words on it, you know it came from a person. In my opinion, this is similar to what happened when scientists discovered DNA; however, the amount of information is far more than just some words on a piece of paper (next point).

Second, the *sheer amount of information in DNA is enormous.* There is way too much information to have come about by chance. The human genome (DNA) consists of two sets of three billion letters.[36] This amount is amazing when you compare it to a book with fifty thousand words or roughly two hundred fifty thousand characters. Try pressing fifty random keys on a keyboard and see whether they produce a meaningful sentence; and obviously this doesn't come close to the billions of letters that reside in your DNA.

If you are wondering whether a very simple organism has much less information and whether DNA could evolve to what humans have today, it doesn't work. Even one of the simplest organisms, a single-celled amoeba, has more information in the cell nucleus than all thirty volumes of the *Encyclopedia Britannica*.[37] Bill Gates, founder of Microsoft, compared DNA to a computer program but said it was far more advanced.[38]

The bottom line is that the information in living organisms is far too large and complex to have originated from random acts of nature. An intelligent designer, God, is far more likely.

What Is a Logical Summary of This Argument?

1. Since information requires intelligence, any information found in the natural world would require a supernatural mind (God).

2. DNA is information in nature that directs the growth of an organism and certain activities (for example, healing).

3. Therefore, a supernatural mind (God) is the best explanation for DNA.

Skeptic: Given Enough Time, Random Natural Forces Will Eventually Produce What Appears to Be Information in DNA

The skeptic will likely contend that, given enough time, DNA could develop from random forces. In other words, if you shake a bunch of molecules together long enough, information in the form of DNA will emerge. But, as already discussed, the nature of information and the vast amount of information make natural forces as the cause of information in DNA extremely unlikely, if not mathematically impossible.

The skeptic may contend that declaring God as the source of DNA is a God-of-the-gaps approach, inserting God as an explanation for the unknown. But this is clearly false. Our conclusion isn't based on what we don't know but rather on what we do know. Based on the nature of information as well as the quantity of information in the DNA of living organisms, we are inferring that it must come from intelligence. This is reasoning to the best explanation (a form of logic called "abductive reasoning").

Is There a Verse in the Bible Related to God Being Our Creator (Which Would Include Information in Our DNA)?

This verse is a psalm from David that glorifies God as the Creator. "I will give thanks to You, for I am fearfully and wonderfully made; Wonderful are Your works, And my soul knows it very well" (Psalm 139:14 NASB).

Summary Point: Information requires intelligence; and since nature is filled with information, it clearly points to a divine intelligence—God.

The next time you see the design of a play (Xs and Os) or a quarterback call an audible (code), perhaps it will remind you that information requires intelligence— supporting the notion that DNA points to God.

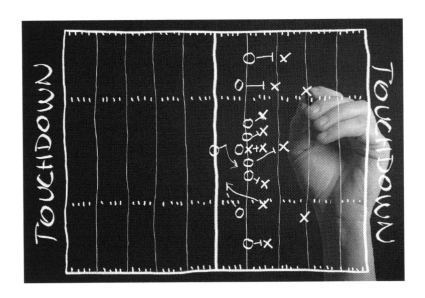

5
Shocking Return

Score:

Chad's team: 17
Adam's team: 7

Time remaining:

Second quarter, forty-four minutes left in the game

I can't believe what I'm seeing. Are my eyes deceiving me? I blink hard, squeezing my eyelids tight; but upon reopening them, the same image is running toward me. Joe, by far our fastest receiver, is running back on the field toward me for the next play.

How can this be? I wonder.

Joe took a vicious hit in the first quarter and hasn't returned since. He was running a crossing route in the middle of the field when his path was suddenly and forcefully interrupted by a linebacker who had read Joe's route. I fired the ball quickly, but just as the football connected with Joe's hands, the linebacker absolutely blasted him. It was like watching someone run into a wall. A violent collision. Joe crumpled to the ground as if all the life had left his body.

When I saw Joe fall, I gasped, sucking in a quick breath of air. My breathing paused, and a pit hit my stomach. My reaction was triggered by deep wounds—the worst memory of my life by far. I remember seeing a lifeless body. My mother.

I was only seven years old, and Mom and I were alone at home. Just a short time earlier, we had finished making a puzzle. Even at a young age, I recognized that she always found a way, in between the busyness of life, to spend time with me.

I had left the room to do something—I don't remember what. When I returned several minutes later, I found my mom lying on the floor, right hand on her chest. Her face was motionless and looking at the ceiling. Her mouth and eyes were open. I remember her eyes. There was no life at all in her eyes. I let out a scream and threw myself at my mom to wake her up. I tried shaking her as tears poured down my face. I yelled for help, but no one was around. I must have called 911, but I don't recall much more about that day. I just remember seeing her lifeless body and wishing she would awaken. She never did.

When Joe was hit in the first quarter, he was on the ground for several minutes—not from a heart attack but from a major collision. Training staff worked on him for some time. Fortunately, he rose and walked slowly off the field. But he didn't remain on the sideline; instead he went straight to the locker room. No one had seen him since the first quarter, and I was certain he was done for the game. But after getting clearance from strict and rigorous testing by the team doctor, he was now back on the field. I am glad he is physically okay, and it is extraordinary that he is able to return.

With everyone now in formation, I settle under center. I scan the defense while barking some fake audibles. *No need to change the play. I like the look. I like our chances.*

With a final shout, I take the snap and quickly drop back seven yards. The line forms a nice pocket, providing time for the play to develop. I look left to my primary target, but the defense plays it well, bracketing the receiver between two defenders. *Not what I was expecting. Their scheme mixed things up and fooled me.*

Fortunately, I have time to adjust. I look back toward the center of the field and see Joe streaking up the middle in a post-pattern, just past the linebackers, who are still backpedaling, failing to keep up. I hesitate for a moment. I didn't intend to throw a pass to Joe on his first play back. I figured I would let him settle back into the game. In fact, his assignment for the play was primarily to be a decoy and drag the safety away from the primary target. But he's open. *He's open!*

I tap the ball with my left hand and lob it high in the middle of the field. A linebacker covering that zone jumps high to knock the pass away, but it sails just over his hand, missing it by only a few inches.

The ball looks to be falling innocently to the ground, a lame-duck pass no one will touch, when Joe comes sprinting across to make the catch. His speed is amazing.

There is a lot of room ahead of Joe. The deep safety is the lone defender between Joe and the end zone, the only one in position to make the tackle or slow him down. But just as the defender takes an angle to close the distance, Joe makes a spectacular cut to the left. The sharp move catches the safety off guard, buckling his ankles.

The rest of the fans who aren't already standing snap to their feet. Joe finishes the play, running down the middle of the field with no one within ten yards.

Touchdown!

We are right back in this game.

I am thankful but shocked that Joe returned to the game.

How Do Injuries in Football Relate to Evidence for Life after Death?

Football is a violent sport. Unfortunately, injuries do occur, but thankfully many are fairly minor, allowing a player to leave the field by his or her own power. However, occasionally injuries are serious, causing players to remain on the ground for some time, or they may leave the game by cart. On rare occasions a player may suffer momentary paralysis or lose consciousness, but almost always that person will come back to play at some point in the future. It's amazing, sometimes shocking, how football players return from serious hits and injuries; and I truly hope that, through technology and rule changes, the sport will continue to become as safe as possible.

But far more extraordinary is when someone suffers a serious medical emergency (for example, a heart attack) to the point that he or she shows signs of death and then returns to life. In some situations, the person may have a near-death experience (NDE), a *return* that is even more shocking than a football player returning from a serious injury. An NDE is a real out-of-body experience in which a person's soul leaves his or her body. If you're skeptical, you may be interested to learn that there is strong evidence for these occurrences. We must be careful about how we interpret what is reported, but the experiences provide a good reason to believe we aren't just our bodies. You have a soul, and life continues after your body dies.

Why Should We Believe NDEs Are Real Out-of-Body Experiences?

There are thousands of NDE reports of real out-of-body experiences (OBEs). Some have seen their physical bodies receiving medical treatment or other events happening on earth. Other experiences include a visit to a spiritual dimension to see deceased relatives and possibly a review of their lives.[39] Some have had a combination of both earthly and spiritual experiences.[40] Why should we believe these are real out-of-body experiences and not lies, dreams, hallucinations, or merely brain activity?

First, there are thousands of reported cases of NDEs, and quite possibly many more are unreported. One particular author on this topic, Jeffrey Long, MD, founder of Near Death Experience Research Foundation (NDERF), has studied thousands of reports. Based on this evidence, he believes without a doubt that there is life after bodily death.[41]

Second, the variety of people reporting similar events includes young children and blind people (including those blind from birth).[42] It's highly unlikely they are all fabricating similar stories, especially children who are less inclined to lie for some benefit.

Third, according to Dr. Michael Sabom, who has researched NDEs extensively, people who have experienced an NDE tend to no longer fear death.[43] It's obvious why; they have seen that life doesn't cease when our bodies die. If they were lying about their NDE, there would be no change in their fear of death.

Fourth, and perhaps most powerful, is the fact that natural explanations fail to account for NDE reports that include experiences the person witnessed far away from his or her body (for example, conversations of family members).[44] There is no way the person could have this information unless he or she truly had an out-of-body experience. Based on the research of hundreds of reports, Jeffrey Long, MD, also confirms the point that people see events that occur far from their bodies as well as people working to resuscitate their physical bodies.[45]

Finally, according to John Burke's *Imagine Heaven*, a book I recommend on this topic, it has been reported that NDEs seem to be more real and vivid than normal experiences.[46]

What Can We Conclude from NDEs?

NDEs seem to provide compelling evidence of life after death. They may be the best proof that when our physical bodies die, that moment isn't the end of our existence. This belief certainly runs contrary to atheism or naturalism, which claims that all we are are our physical bodies.

Nonetheless, we should be careful about drawing specific religious conclusions from NDE reports.[47] People may have real experiences, but how they interpret them could be swayed by their personal bias. In other words, they may really see an angelic being but could wrongly interpret it as the god of their choice.

Skeptics: Isn't It More Likely That NDEs Involve Seeing a Vision, Hallucination, or Simply Some Brain Activity, Not a Real Out-of-Body Experience?

No. This isn't a good response for at least two reasons.

First, many accounts have accurately described people and events while they were being treated medically. Given their state of unconsciousness, there is no way they could know these things.

Second, as discussed, some people who have had NDEs *witnessed events far away from their bodies,* descriptions that were later verified as accurate. Consequently, there is no way NDEs can be some brain event, triggered by drugs or part of the natural dying process. Even if some drugs can trigger visions, NDE events are different. They are real experiences.

Does the Bible Support the Notion of NDEs?

Although there are no definitive references to NDEs, the Bible is clear that we have immaterial souls, which make NDEs possible.

Additionally, the apostle Paul made a reference that supports the possibility of out-of-body experiences. It has been suggested that the following could be Paul referring to an NDE he may have experienced:[48] "I know a man in Christ who was caught up into the third heaven 14 years ago. Whether he was in the body or out of the body, I don't know; God knows. I know that this man-whether in the body or out of the body I do not know, God knows- was caught up into paradise. He heard inexpressible words, which a man is not allowed to speak" (2 Corinthians 12:2–4 HCSB).

This quotation certainly could have been describing a vision, but it's interesting that Paul says the man could be in the body or out of the body. His words clearly support the possibility of NDEs.

Summary Point: Near-death experiences provide strong evidence that there is life after the death of our bodies.

The next time you see a seriously injured player return to play football, perhaps it will remind you that many people have returned from near-death experiences, proving there is life after physical death.

6
Free Will

Score:

Chad's team: 24
Adam's team: 14

Time remaining:

Second quarter: Thirty-nine minutes left in the game

Fourth down in our own territory. Usually punting is a no-brainer, but with only one yard to go, we have a decision to make. Chad's team answered our last score with a touchdown and has a ten-point lead again, adding pressure to the decision.

The snow is heavier now and starting to stick to the ground. There's not much accumulation yet but enough to be a factor. The crowd is cheering for us go for it. There is hesitation from our sideline, but then Coach holds up his hands for the offense to stay on the field. We're going for it!

I get the play call from the sideline. Our biggest running back, Moe, sprints in from the sideline and enters the huddle. I scan the eyes of each offensive player, trying to show confidence.

"All right guys." I look left. "Option Right—Exodus 314." I turn to the right. "Option Right—Exodus 314," I say, repeating the play to the other side of the huddle.

"On one. On one." The last instruction lets everyone know when the ball is to be snapped, a quick snap to catch the defense off guard. "Readyyyyy. Break!" We clap in unison to break the huddle and head to the line of scrimmage.

Everyone quickly runs to his assigned position. I settle in under center, scanning the defense. *Really starting to snow now. Not sure about this play if the ground is slippery.*

The defensive line is crammed in tight, filling the A and B gaps, expecting a run up the middle. Although I was initially hoping for a passing play, this play might work against what the defense seems to be anticipating.

"Ready," I bark loudly. "Set. Go!"

The ball snaps sharply into my hands. I take an extra moment to make sure I have the wet pigskin. The defense might not have been expecting such a quick snap, but they react quickly, crashing into the line of scrimmage. The sounds of helmets colliding and the grunting of players battling each other fill the field.

I shift to the right and let the fullback run past me. I hide the ball in my right hand, sticking my left hand in his belly, hoping the linebackers will either hesitate or attack our decoy. The fullback slams into the middle of the line of scrimmage, his arms pressed against his stomach as if he is cradling the ball.

The defense penetrates the gaps, blowing up the offensive line. I run horizontally down the right side of the line of scrimmage. I am looking for an opening to lunge for one yard, but it's a wall of colliding bodies. I'm shadowed by Moe, who is also running down the line of scrimmage about five yards behind me, mirroring my position. It's a classic option play.

As I get past the wall of bodies, space opens, and it's decision time. The play allows me to decide to tuck the ball away and run myself or pitch to Moe, who is shadowing me about five yards behind. Usually the defense will dictate the decision, but sometimes, it's a fifty-fifty call, and I need to make a split-second decision. This is one of those times. Free will.

Sometimes I really hate making decisions.

I remember making a fifty-fifty decision in high school—not about grades but about Elliana, a girl I had been eyeing for some time. Her physical appearance was captivating. Long brown hair and hazel eyes. A smile that could warm your heart. Short and slender. She was beautiful. But she was more than that. Her heart and integrity separated her from the crowd. She followed her own path, caring little about what the cool kids thought. I was drawn to her in so many ways.

School was ending, and my time was running out. I would need to make a move or risk Elliana becoming a fond memory. It was a Friday in June, and class was over. People were exiting the building, and I saw Elliana walking my direction. I felt panic run through my body. Butterflies filled my stomach. I wanted to say something but didn't dare look at her. Instead I let her stroll past me.

It was at that point when I felt like I had a fifty-fifty decision. Do I say something and risk rejection? Or go for it? Two seconds of indecision seemed like five minutes of agony. I needed to decide.

"Elliana?" I turned and called, my voice filled with hope.

"Yes?"

She responded! It was already a small victory, but there was still plenty of room for defeat. I stepped forward to close the distance so other kids walking past wouldn't hear me make a fool of myself. Her expression seemed inviting enough.

"I … I … Do you like mini golf?"

Where did that come from? I thought. I guess I should have spent more time rehearsing what I was going to say.

"Sure," she responded with a smile that was even more affirming than her words. Her eyes glimmered, and I almost forgot it was my turn to say something.

"Would you like to play sometime?" I asked. A moment later, I added, "With me?" I included the second part just in case, you know, there was any question.

"I would love to."

Her response was music to my ears. We set a date and played mini golf, which she won. It was the start of something special. To think it came down to one moment of free will. If I had decided differently, life wouldn't be the same.

But now a much different decision is at hand. I need to make a decision on this critical option play. The wrong choice will give the ball back to my brother's team and could lead to defeat.

Since I need to get upfield only a few yards, I could secure the ball and run—maybe dive for the first down. The danger is that there are a lot of defenders close by.

The other option is to pitch the ball to Moe, who has more room, but he is five yards behind me and needs to cover more ground to get the first down. Also, what if the ball picks up some snow in the air and slips through his hands?

Decide. Decide!

I decide to take it myself. I turn upfield but am quickly surprised by an adversary before getting back to the line of scrimmage. A linebacker who was hidden behind a wall of large players appears in my path. He lowers his shoulder into my gut, stopping all my forward momentum. I'm certain I didn't get far enough for the first down. My right foot slips out from the snow, and I start falling back.

About to be slammed to the ground, I make a bold and dangerous, maybe dumb, decision. With my right arm free, I toss the ball back to where I think Moe should be; I don't have time to turn my head and check before the risky lateral. It could be a good play or disaster.

I hit the ground with a thud and flash a look to the right to see Moe grab the ball out of the air.

It is all on you now.

Moe turns up the field quickly. With most of the defense in the middle of the field, there are only a couple of defenders for him to worry about, but they are closing quickly.

As part of the play, the wide receiver from the far right comes crashing down the line to block the incoming safety. They both go low; the collision is a stalemate. That leaves Moe one-on-one with the cornerback, who unfortunately is in a prime position to grab him until help arrives.

Suddenly out of nowhere, our tight end, who released from the line of scrimmage, comes flying in and levels the cornerback from the side. He absolutely blasts him. The defender crumples under the fierce block. The two blockers have crisscrossed, opening a path for Moe that never should have been there.

With virtually everyone else near the line of scrimmage, Moe gallops down the sideline to the promised land, scoring our third touchdown.

It is amazing how we went from certain defeat to a wide-open path for the touchdown.

I wonder, *Can we keep up this momentum and take the lead?*

My freewill decision was wrong; fortunately, Moe saved me.

How Does an Option Play Relate to Evidence for God?

Your ability to think and make decisions is best explained by a soul, your immaterial being. This is because there is no combination of material things in nature (for example, atoms) that could enable humans to have consciousness, free will, or the ability to reason.

In football, coaches and players think and make decisions all the time. A coach analyzes the situation and examines the playbook to make the right call. A quarterback may run an option play or drop back and pick a receiver to throw the ball to. Sometimes the choice is obvious based on the opposition, but other times there are multiple options that seem to be of similar value, and a difficult decision must be made.

If you don't have a soul, you are merely a robot made of living tissue. Free will is an illusion. Your genetics reacting to the environment around you completely dictate your decisions.

But deep down we all know this isn't the case. We may have certain tendencies, but you are different from a robot programmed to act in a certain way. You truly have freedom to make decisions and take different actions. Physical elements of the body cannot explain this fact. Philosopher J. P. Moreland makes the point that consciousness and thinking couldn't have evolved from matter.[49] They are both immaterial activities.

A soul is the best explanation for your consciousness (awareness of self), free will (making decisions), and ability to reason; and since a soul is immaterial it makes sense that it was created by an immaterial being, God, who connected it to a physical body.

Why Is God the Best Explanation for the Existence of Logic, which Enables Us to Reason?

We all use logic. Logic provides rules for clear thinking, the right way to reason. Even if we don't formally study logic, we all know there is a right and wrong way to reason. Consider the following example:

1. If it rains during the football game, the ball will be slippery.
2. It is raining during the game.
3. Therefore, the ball will be slippery.

The conclusion is obvious based on points one and two. There is a technical name for this if-then rule in logic, but you don't need to know it to understand how to reason. It is wired into you.

It would obviously be irrational if we changed number three to "Therefore, the home team will win," because the premises (numbers one and two) wouldn't align with that conclusion. If someone were to try to reason this way, we would say he or she was wrong. This is because the rules of logic are objective; they exist independently of the opinions of mankind.

When we follow the rules of logic, we are being rational, and when we violate them, we are being irrational. These rules cannot be changed; they transcend mankind. They are also immaterial, since you cannot see or touch these rules.

Since logic provides rules that are immaterial and universal to all mankind (objective), they cannot be explained by nature (material); nor are they simply man-made rules.[50]

Consider two points. First, the source must be beyond nature (transcendent). Second, since they involve rational thinking, they are best explained by a mind. Put these two points together, and the existence of logic is best explained by a transcendent mind—God.

You don't need to believe in God to use logic, but without God, there wouldn't be an adequate explanation for the existence of logic.

How Does Free Will Relate to God's Being Seemingly Hidden?

Someone may ask why God isn't more obvious about His existence. How could a good God remain seemingly hidden from His creation, especially if our salvation depends on our beliefs about Him? Let me offer two responses, one of which includes free will.

First, the Bible is clear that everyone knows God exists. "For since the creation of the world God's invisible qualities—his eternal power and divine nature—have been clearly seen, being understood from what has been made, so that people are without excuse" (Romans 1:20 NIV). Some people suppress this truth[51] for a variety of reasons. They may not want to follow God's rules, instead choosing to pursue their own desires. Or perhaps they blame God for emotional scars they carry. God may not be visible, but evidence for His existence isn't hidden; rather, some people suppress the truth of God's existence.

Second, God may not be overtly obvious about His existence to allow people to have free will to decide whether to follow God.[52] *God wants us to love Him, not simply be aware that He exists.* If God made His existence obvious, more people would believe He exists and follow His commands, but they may not genuinely love God. God wants not only our minds but also our hearts.

Consider the following situation. You are at work, and no one else is around. You could take a longer lunch or leave work a little early without anyone knowing. You get to decide whether to follow the rules. You have freedom to choose. However, if your manager were around, you would follow all the rules, not necessarily by choice to do what is right but rather by fear of punishment.[53]

Similarly, if you were aware of God standing over your shoulder, His presence may override your free will.[54] Consequently, perhaps God isn't overtly obvious about His existence to allow you to make a freewill decision to pursue Him.

In this part of the football story, the option play included Adam's fake to the fullback and hiding the ball. There was a purpose or reason for the hiddenness. It was to deceive the defense, using a play-action fake. But God's hiddenness is different. He isn't looking to deceive us at all but rather to allow us to make a genuine choice for Him. By removing Himself, God provides an opportunity for people to choose God with their hearts. Perhaps the next time you see a play-action fake (quarterback fakes a handoff to a running back while hiding the ball in his other hand), it will remind you that God has reasons for His apparent hiddenness.

Skeptic: Doesn't the Brain Provide the Ability to Think, Reason, and Make Decisions?

There is a big difference between your brain and mind. Your mind is who you are, providing the ability to think and make decisions, while your brain is the conduit between your mind and body. Your mind decides to move your arm, and consequently your brain sends electric impulses through your body to accomplish this movement.

How do we know that the mind and brain aren't the same? Let's discuss two reasons.

First, they have different attributes. Mental events aren't the same as physical activities taking place in the brain. Brain activity is visible (for example, electrical impulses), while mind activity isn't (for example, images and thoughts of the mind cannot be seen). Brain activity has physical properties, such as the location and weight of electrical impulses, while mental events, our thoughts, don't have any physical characteristics.[55]

Second, scientific experiments have proved that brain activity cannot make a person believe or decide to do something. Wilder Penfield, a neurosurgeon, mapped the human brain by electrically shocking certain areas of the brain of conscious patients; this probing caused certain physical movements, but Penfield admitted that electrical stimulation wouldn't cause a person to believe something or make a decision.[56] Consequently, it isn't simply brain activity that accounts for thinking, believing, and deciding.

The brain and mind interact with each other (mental events cause brain activity), but they aren't exactly the same.

But someone may ask, "Doesn't brain damage that impacts your memory and ability to think prove your mind and brain are the same?" Not necessarily. It may be that if your brain is damaged, it may impact the ability to think and remember because the receiver (the brain) has been damaged; perhaps this is similar to a damaged radio not being able to receive signals to play music.

Overall, since matter and energy cannot think or make decisions, atheism lacks an adequate explanation to account for free will and thinking; but an immaterial soul accounts for these activities.

Are There Bible Verses That Support the Existence of a Soul, the Notion of Free Will, and the Ability to Reason?

Absolutely, let's look at some of them.

There are a number of verses in the Bible that mention the human soul. For example, in the Genesis account of creation, God created the human body and then breathed life into it, which is our soul. "Then the Lord God formed man of dust from the ground, and breathed into his nostrils the breath of life; and man became a living being" (Genesis 2:7 NASB).

In the New Testament, Jesus made a sharp distinction between the body and the soul. "Do not be afraid of those who kill the body but cannot kill the soul. Rather, be afraid of the One who can destroy both soul and body in hell" (Matthew 10:28 NIV).

The idea of free will is consistent with the Bible. In fact, in the verse below, Jesus confirmed that we have a will that is different from His will (He wanted to gather them, but people within Jerusalem were not willing). "'Jerusalem, Jerusalem! The city who kills the prophets and stones those who are sent to her. How often I wanted to gather your children together, as a hen gathers her chicks under her wings, but you were not willing!'" (Luke 13:34 HCSB).

Finally, in the book of Isaiah, God told us to reason with Him; so clearly we get our ability to think from our Creator. "*'Come now, and let us reason together,' Says the Lord*, 'Though your sins are as scarlet, They will be as white as snow; Though they are red like crimson, They will be like wool'" (Isaiah 1:18 NASB, emphasis added).

Summary Point: God is the best explanation for logic (immaterial rules for reasoning) and our immaterial souls, which enable us to have free will and the ability to think and reason.

The next time you see an option play, such as a Run-Pass-Option (picture below), or really any football player make a decision, perhaps it will remind you that a soul explains your ability to think, reason, and have free will.

7
Good Reasons

Score:

>Chad's team: 24
>Adam's team: 21

Time remaining:

>Second quarter, 33 minutes left in the game

It's just before halftime, and we finally have the ball with a chance to take the lead. We have been fighting an uphill battle during the entire first half; it's been emotionally draining.

Their defense has been vicious. Many times when I have dropped back to pass, I've taken some kind of hit. One time I lost hearing briefly, except for a twang—a real case of getting my bell rung. At this rate, I'm wondering whether my body will allow me to make it through the game.

As my team forms a huddle, I look to the sideline for instruction. When I get the signal from the coaches, I let out a slight grin. *Great play call. The perfect antidote for an aggressive defense.*

I settle in under center, trying to look normal and not give away the surprise. I see the eyes of a defensive lineman staring back at me. He has the look of a ferocious dog, waiting for the ball to move so he can chase down and devour a slab of raw meat—me.

I take the snap and drop back several yards. In less than two seconds, there are three defenders who are free and bearing down on me. I continue backpedaling to buy some extra time.

The defensive tackle whom I locked eyes with before the play is closing quickly. He is huge, weighing at least one hundred pounds more than I do. He reaches out and grabs my jersey, yanking me toward him as I try to pull away. I'm no match for his strength. I'm about to get flattened but am able to flick my wrist, tossing a pass about ten yards to the right. A small, speedy running back, Dave, is waiting for the ball. He has a convoy of offensive linemen, who purposely released their defenders to set up the play. I am the bait.

It's a perfect screen pass play, allowing the defense to penetrate to set up blockers for Dave. Unfortunately, I was just a moment late with the pass, and my behemoth opponent, already in the process of driving me to the ground, finishes the task. He must weigh over three hundred pounds, and his body lands directly on me. My ribs buckle almost to the point of breaking. The air in my lungs is forced out like someone stomped on a whoopee cushion. A bolt of electricity shoots up my spine, ending at the back of my neck. I feel like a car at the junkyard getting crushed.

My thoughts try to console my physical body, reminding me that there is a purpose to all this physical pain I'm absorbing. There's no question I would rather have physical pain than emotional pain. The former always seems to heal more quickly. I have never fully recovered from my mom's death.

But somewhere along the way, my emotional pain started to turn to intellectual questions. What is the meaning of life? If there is a God, as some claim, why does God allow evil and suffering? Certainly God has the power to fix the world, right? I wasn't wondering anymore because of my emotional scars; rather I was trying to make sense of why certain things happen.

Elliana is a Christian, and she encouraged me to speak to her pastor. I wanted to roll my eyes, but instead I hid my skepticism from her. I decided to meet with the pastor anyway. What could it hurt?

We met for breakfast, his treat. He sipped his coffee as he listened to my story. His posture and eyes told me he genuinely cared about what I had to say.

After a lot of listening, he talked about a fallen world that is currently reaping the consequences of rebellion against God; but His Son was sent to die for our sins and save us from eternal judgment if we accept this gift of grace. I had heard this story about Jesus from Elliana. He assured me that God truly cares about people and their circumstances, like the pain I was experiencing; we should pursue God with our heart and pray for spiritual comfort as well as seek support from family and friends.

But this wasn't enough for me. I no longer needed support for my emotional pain; I wanted answers. The pastor responded with a tough question. "What do you think God's role is in our life?"

I hesitated. *Why are you asking me?* I thought. *Shouldn't you have that answer?* I shrugged my shoulders and raised my eyebrows. I had no answer.

The pastor broke the silence. "Many people think God is there for our requests when we need Him. In other words, He is there to make our lives comfortable and answer our prayers. For example, please heal my uncle, find me a new job, take away this pain in my back, protect my children from any and all harm, et cetera. It is true that God cares very much for us, and we should definitely bring our requests to Him; but we should also understand that God is more concerned about our eternal destination than about making our life on earth comfortable and fun."

I gave him a quick "Hmm." His words seemed to make some sense. I took my last bite of home fries and returned my eyes to his so he knew I was attentive.

He continued, "Bad things happen because mankind disobeyed God and the world is fallen. Corrupted. It wasn't God's original creation, but it's our fault and our reality. Now God could stop all bad things from happening, but that would start with taking away our free will."[57]

The pastor's right hand motioned around the diner. "Each person is allowed to make choices, good or bad. Free will is very important to God. It's necessary to have genuine love relationships, including with our Creator. It's actually why hell exists, because people are free to reject God. Evil cannot be extinguished without taking away free will."

"Okay," I interjected. I had something to stump him. "That makes some sense, I guess, but what about pain and suffering that doesn't come from people? Like earthquakes? Disease? Sickness?" I didn't want to mention my mom's heart attack. I wanted an answer without getting emotional.

"That's a great question. Again, those things exist because we live in a world that is corrupted by our rebellion. It's our fault that death and suffering entered creation. You may still wonder why God doesn't just change the world back to peace. It goes back to my point that God is far more concerned about eternity. God is justified in allowing something bad to happen on earth if it's possible that there is an eternal benefit."

The pastor paused and looked up as if searching for the next few words. "If some event brings pain or suffering, even despair, but could later lead to a change in someone's heart and eventually eternal salvation, shouldn't God allow it?"

He wiped his mouth with the napkin in his lap and leaned forward, as if this point was especially important. "Or maybe challenging circumstances in our life might help develop our soul. I know that I have grown the most spiritually when going through difficult situations. This can be tough for us to understand because we may not know what the potential benefit is. Also, it may be for us or someone else. But we should trust that God has good reasons for allowing pain and suffering, even if unknown to us."

The pastor paused and looked at me intently. "This is a very difficult topic, and I don't mean to make it sound easy. It's probably the most challenging question. I have shared some answers, but I don't want you to lose sight that God loves you. You are His child, and He is there for you."

I don't know whether I was fully convinced, but he gave me something to think about. Also, what really struck me was the discussion we had about atheism. If there is no God, then there is no eternal purpose to life or suffering. Atheism doesn't seem to solve anything—it seems to make it worse. The conversation left me feeling a bit hollow, empty inside about my current worldview.

As we left the diner, I thanked the pastor for his time and extended my hand for a closing shake. With all the struggles in my life, I was glad he'd shared some possible reasons for God allowing evil.

Oddly enough, the conversation now reminds me that there was also a reason for allowing the defense to penetrate and attack me; it was part of the design of the play. However, my body is absorbing more punishment than I prefer. *At least I got the pass off.*

Dave extends his hands and catches the football with ease. He takes half a second to make sure he has the ball and then spins 180 degrees to turn upfield. He has a nice escort to run down the right sideline. The play is set up nicely.

The three offensive linemen rumble downfield, zeroing in on defenders that need to be neutralized. The first two linemen collectively pancake a small defender, who seems to prefer hitting the ground rather than a direct confrontation. They smother him anyway, ensuring he is completely out of the play.

Dave is right behind the last blocker with two defenders to beat. He reaches out his hand to touch the back of the giant lineman, staying close to his human shield. The closest defender has no choice but to pick a side. He tries to run around the left side, but the lineman extends his arms and launches his body, pushing the defender several yards away.

Dave has one man to beat for a touchdown.

Dave is fast but not quick enough to avoid the final defender, who is much bigger and bearing down on him. With the sideline close by, Dave has little room to make any moves. Instead he makes a quick decision to take him head on, extending his hand into the defender's facemask. The stiff arm catches the defensive player off guard, snapping his head backward. He was expecting Dave to try to beat him with quickness.

Dave has all the leverage. The defender is so off balance he is actually falling backward. He grabs Dave's jersey in an attempt to drag him down with him. Dave is now falling forward but removes his left hand from the defender's facemask and extends it to the ground to stop his momentum and stay on his feet. The defender grasps at Dave's feet as they trample the larger adversary, but he isn't able to wrap up the tackle.

Dave has completely run over the larger defender. He stumbles another few yards before standing up right and accelerating forward. He scampers down the sideline with no one else in sight.

Touchdown!

But wait. Why is the defense clapping? That makes no sense.

Then I see the yellow handkerchief on the ground, and my heart sinks. We committed a penalty, negating our score.

You have to be kidding me!

I force my aching body to stand upright in time to see the referee give the hand signals, making it official—holding on the offense.

We enter halftime on the losing end of the scoreboard. What will the next thirty minutes of game time bring?

We had our reasons for allowing the defense to attack, and although the play worked, our penalty had consequences.

How Does a Screen Pass Help Explain How God Can Allow Evil to Exist in the World?

Some football plays purposely allow the defense to attack and penetrate the offense as part of the design of the play. Initially the play may seem bad for the offense, but then it becomes clear that it was *allowed* for a reason, to set up a successful play.

Similarly, *God allows evil to exist in the world because of an ultimate good reason.* The challenge for us, as finite beings with limited knowledge, is that we may not know what that good reason is; suffering may seem meaningless based on our limited knowledge.[58] It may be intended to benefit us or someone else.

If you or someone you know is suffering, this answer may seem harsh and uncaring. *What possible good reason could God have for allowing my situation?* Intellectual answers aren't appropriate when someone is suffering emotionally. During these times we should pursue God and seek His help and comfort as well as support from family and friends.

However, if you have an intellectual question about the problem of evil and suffering, there are some valid responses worth considering. Let's discuss them further.

What Is the Problem of Evil?

The problem of evil contends that if God exists and is all good and all powerful, He wouldn't allow evil and suffering in the world. But since there is evil in the world, God must not exist.

Christianity can offer two responses:

1. There is compelling evidence that God *does* exist (as discussed in earlier chapters).
2. There are good reasons why God allows evil and suffering (see below).

What Is Evil?

From a Christian perspective, evil isn't a substance or thing; rather, it is the corruption or lack of something that was intended to be good.[59] For example, being blind isn't a specific thing but rather the inability to see, the lack of something good. A football example might be a crack in a helmet. The crack isn't something in and of itself, but rather it is something bad that happened to the helmet. God didn't create evil; rather, mankind's rebellion corrupted the world. Sickness, disease, and natural disasters became part of creation (natural evil). Humans inherited a sinful nature, a bent toward selfish desires, which may lead to actions that are contrary to God's moral standard (moral evil).

The Christian definition of evil makes sense because it defines evil as objective, violating a standard of goodness independent of people's opinions. The evil and suffering we witness may sicken us, but we don't decide or change what is considered evil.

Other worldviews struggle to provide a reasonable explanation of evil. Atheism generally contends that evil is subjective; whatever people or societies decide is wrong. But this isn't true; we know there are some evils that are heinous (for example, genocide or domestic abuse) regardless of people's opinions. Some religions view evil as an illusion, which is difficult to understand; sickness, theft, and murder aren't illusions.

What Are Possible Christian Responses for Why God May Allow Evil and Suffering to Occur?

There are various possible reasons, but let's discuss three: free will, greater good, and character development. Again, these responses aren't appropriate for anyone who may be struggling emotionally; rather, they are intended to offer potential responses from an intellectual perspective.

The most common response is free will. God allows every person genuine freedom to make good or bad decisions. Some people make selfish decisions that cause harm to others (moral evil). For God to truly stop all moral evil in the world, He would need to remove everyone's free will.[60] However, free will is necessary to have genuine love, which is what God desires from His creation.

Another possible reason is that God has *a greater good* that supersedes the evil and suffering that are allowed to occur. One example is eternal salvation. God's primary purpose for our earthly lives isn't happiness but rather for people to freely choose to love and follow God and to go to heaven.[61] God is justified in allowing evil or suffering in the world if brokenness may cause people to freely turn to Him. Moreover, according to Dr. Clay Jones, a good reason for allowing evil is that people are being prepared for God's kingdom by coming to understand the horror of rebelling against God and learning to overcome evil with good.[62]

Finally, God may allow suffering or evil to occur if it will benefit our character.[63] Sometimes we experience more spiritual growth when we go through hard times. People tend to spend much more time praying and seeking God in times of need, which may strengthen our relationship with Him.

Skeptic: It Is Ridiculous to Suggest God Has Good Reasons for Allowing Evil. Tell That to Someone Who Has Lost a Child to Cancer or Been Violently Abused

Based on the tone, this approach tries to mix the emotional side with the intellectual objection. Although our emotions are important, they need to be distinguished from the intellectual challenge. The responses offered above are potential good reasons to the intellectual question of why God may allow evil and suffering. Given all the positive evidence for God's existence, we should trust that God has good reasons for allowing evil even if it's unknown to us.

Additionally, skeptics must offer an explanation for what evil is and why it exists. Based on their worldview, they will struggle to explain objective evil, which supports the notion that certain actions are evil regardless of the opinions of mankind. To have an objective standard of good and evil, a transcendent source (God) is required.

Finally, skeptics may counter that, just because God may exist, why is God necessarily good? Could God be evil? A powerful being could be evil, but if God is the ultimate perfect being, then God is necessarily good because *goodness is superior to evil.*

Are There Bible Verses to Support the Reasons Above?

Free will is a concept clearly taught in the Bible. The previous chapter provided a scripture verse regarding free will, so let's look at the other points in this chapter.

Regarding the notion that God has ultimate good reasons for allowing evil, consider the story of Joseph in the book of Genesis. His envious brothers sold him into slavery and lied to their father about his death. But Joseph rose to a prominent position in Egypt and was reunited with his brothers when they were in danger of famine. Below is Joseph's response when he explained to his brothers why God had allowed them to treat him harshly. "But Joseph said to them, 'Don't be afraid. Am I in the place of God? You planned evil against me; God planned it for good to bring about the present result—the survival of many people'" (Genesis 50:19–20 HCSB).

Moreover, in the book of Acts, God allowed Stephen, a follower of Christ, to be stoned, a clear act of evil. But this stoning was followed by persecution and the scattering of Christians, which led to the message of salvation being preached in other areas of the world (an eternal benefit). "Saul agreed with putting him to death. On that day a severe persecution broke out against the church in Jerusalem, and all except the apostles were scattered throughout the land of Judea and Samaria ... So those who were scattered went on their way proclaiming the message of good news" (Acts 8:1, 4 HCSB). Both examples demonstrate that God will allow evil to occur if there is a greater good.

Finally, the Bible teaches that suffering can benefit our souls. "Not only so, but we also glory in our sufferings, because we know that suffering produces perseverance; perseverance, character; and character, hope" (Romans 5:3–4 NIV).

Summary Point: God cares deeply for mankind and has good reasons for allowing pain and evil in the world. These include granting mankind free will and allowing certain situations that may have an eternal benefit.

The next time you see a play that purposely allows the defense to attack for an ultimate good outcome (such as a screen pass), perhaps it will remind you that God has good reasons for allowing pain and suffering in the world.

8
Not Possible

Score:

> Chad's team: 24
> Adam's team: 21

Time remaining:

> End of halftime, thirty minutes left in the game

My cleats click along the concrete, echoing in the tunnel. Halftime is over, and we're headed back to the field. I stroll along by myself, deep in thought about the task at hand. In thirty minutes the game will be over, leaving me in euphoria or misery. The magnitude of what is at stake, especially for me, is overwhelming. I may look calm on the outside, but my inside is filled stress. Chaos almost. *Good thing I hide it well.*

As my team spills back onto the field, I hear a few cheers sprinkled throughout the stadium. When I reach my designated spot to stretch and throw some warm-up passes, I look up at the scoreboard—21–24. Chad's team is winning by three points. Even though my team had more yards in the first half as well as more plays and a higher time of possession, there is only one measure that really matters—the score.

I notice snow blowing around the field. No real accumulation. Just wind carrying frozen water particles though the air, hiding some of the green grass.

I look up at the sky, which is now dark. Snow is no longer falling. My gaze upward triggers a memory. When I was a young boy, I looked up into the sky, wondering whether Mom was somewhere. Was heaven real? Was she there? Would I see her again? I used to stare intently at the stars, looking for a clue, seeking some sign that this place, which so many people assumed was real, did in fact exist.

Although my heart liked the idea that she was in a better place, I still had moments of wonder and doubt. I wanted to assume the best, but my mind wouldn't allow me to rest and *assume* it was true. I needed more certainty. Mom believed in God, but I kept asking myself, *Does God exist? If so, which one?* I'm not one for blind faith. I'm skeptical by nature.

The field is filled with players from both teams. Stretching. Throwing. Catching. Kicking. Warming up in preparation for the final thirty minutes of battle. But I don't see Chad. He seems to be missing. My eyes keep searching. I can't see all the faces in the helmets; I'm simply checking jersey numbers.

I rescan all the places I have already checked. Where is he? Is it possible he got an injury and won't play in the second half? I don't know whether to be happy or concerned.

Finally, I see him emerge from his team's tunnel. With no helmet on, he is easy to spot. I'm relieved and disappointed. *Chad looks happy. Why is he so happy?* I am filled with anxiety. *Shouldn't he share my stress? Why is he so calm? It's as if he knows something I don't.*

"Adam!" a familiar voice says from my right. I recognize that deep tone. John is an assistant coach on the other team and a friend. I say *friend* for the lack of a better word. We don't hang out, but he has always showed a personal interest in my well-being. Maybe my brother sends him along to periodically check up on me.

"Not sure I want to be chatting with the enemy," I say with a smirk.

John holds up his hands and flashes a smile. "Only wanted to say hello and wish you a good second half. But not too good. You were awesome in the first half. I think you have more passing yards than our total yards."

"The score is the only thing that matters," I reply with a hint of sarcasm, looking up again at the scoreboard.

There is a pause as John also shifts his attention to the scoreboard. "Hmm ... too bad there's only going to be one winner." We exchange a few more pleasantries. Then John waves his right hand, signaling goodbye, as he turns to jog back to his sideline.

The reality of the situation continues to grip me. *I could lose this game.* Obviously, I knew that before, but it is really hitting me now. A new level of panic sends a hot flash through my body, along with a sense of nausea. Despite freezing temperatures, I feel drops of sweat emerge on my forehead. My right hand wipes most of them away before the biting cold can crystalize them. Usually anger consumes my emotions, but my fear is getting stronger. I cannot be at my best if I'm scared, but the possibility of losing now terrorizes me.

I must win this game.

There's only one measure that determines the winner.

How Does the Score of a Football Game Relate to Life after Death?

In football, there are a lot of statistics that measure performance. Either team might have the edge on different statistics, but when the game clock expires, only one measure determines the winner—the final score.

Just as there aren't multiple ways to win a game, there aren't multiple ways to go to heaven (the belief that all religions are true is called "religious pluralism").[64] It may be popular today to say all religions are different paths to the same destination (heaven), but this is not possible. It's impossible because different religions have fundamental beliefs that contradict each other; these aren't just secondary issues but core beliefs that contradict.[65] There is no way for contradicting beliefs to both be true. This violates a fundamental law of logic; two statements that contradict cannot both be true.[66]

Moreover, the sincerity of our beliefs has no bearing on whether something is true. Truth is what corresponds to reality.[67] For example, if I sincerely believe I have $1 million in the bank but really have only $100, my sincerity won't change the truth. Likewise, when we die, the sincerity of our belief won't change our destiny if we choose the wrong path.

Initially, this statement might sound unloving and intolerant, but that isn't my intent. This is about being rational and logical about an extremely important topic. To sugarcoat it with something (pluralism) that violates logic is not only irrational but also unloving.

What Are Some Fundamental Religious Beliefs That Contradict?

1. **Existence of God**: Atheists contend that there is no god and no life after death, beliefs that directly contradict those of many religions. Both sides cannot be right. Someone is wrong. Either God exists, or He doesn't. Either there is life after death, or there isn't.

2. **Jesus's Identity**: A fundamental belief for Christians is that Jesus is God, who descended in the form of a man, while other religions maintain that Jesus isn't God but rather only a human teacher or prophet. That's a clear contradiction; both sides cannot be right. This isn't a secondary issue for Christians; Jesus's identity as God is essential doctrine.

3. **Salvation**: How do we get to heaven? Again, there are contradictory beliefs. According to Christianity, there is only one way to heaven—Jesus. You cannot get to heaven by doing good deeds or worshipping another god; only by the sacrifice of Jesus will God forgive your sins. This belief contradicts other religions, all of which have their separate

views about salvation. Is Christianity's view regarding salvation an exclusive one? See below.

Jesus was very clear about the exclusive path to salvation. Consider the following Bible verse from the Gospel of John. "Jesus told him, 'I am the way, the truth, and the life. No one comes to the Father except through Me'" (John 14:6 HCSB). This isn't the only Bible verse that speaks directly to salvation being exclusive. Consider the words of the apostle Peter. "This [Jesus] is The stone despised by you builders, who has become the cornerstone. There is salvation in no one else, for there is no other name under heaven given to people by which we must be saved" (Acts 4:11–12 HCSB).

Skeptic: The Skeptic May Argue That This View Is Intolerant.
How Dare You Take Such an Intolerant and Exclusive Position!

But this position has nothing to do with tolerance. It has to do with being rational. As already discussed, it isn't possible for contradictions to both be true.

We have personal preferences when it comes to subjective matters, such as favorite foods, music, movies, and so forth. In these examples, the truth resides within each of us. But this doesn't apply to religion. We don't *determine* the truth about God; we *discover* the truth about God.

Tolerance is about treating people fairly when you don't agree with them, not accepting everyone's beliefs as true. I agree that we should respect everyone's free will to choose, but it isn't rational to accept contradictions as true.

Finally, it isn't loving to accept everyone's belief as true if you strongly believe his or her eternal destination is in danger. To accept someone's beliefs as true with the possibility of his or her eternal punishment is unloving. We should treat everyone with respect but not fall into the trap that everyone's beliefs about the afterlife are all true.

Jason M. Jolin

Summary Point: Although it may seem polite to say all religions lead to heaven, this claim isn't logically possible, since each worldview and religion has core beliefs that are in direct contradiction to each other.

The next time you see the score or other statistics for a game, perhaps it will remind you that there is only one measure in football that determines a winner—the score; and, there is only one truth about God that determines our eternal destination.

9

Reliable and True

Score:

    Chad's team: 24
    Adam's team: 21

Time remaining:

    Third quarter, eighteen minutes left in the game

This is one of those defining moments in a game. We are deep in the opposition's territory, in position to kick a field goal and tie the score, so I have to be careful not to make a mistake. But we have a rare opportunity to take our first lead. Third down. Eight yards for a first down; fifteen yards for a touchdown. *I really want a touchdown.*

I'm in shotgun position, flanked by a running back to my left. The crowd is howling. The temperature with the wind is biting cold. I cup my hands to my mouth and blow warm air onto my fingers that are starting to freeze. I point to my right, signaling the slot receiver that it's time to go in motion. He sprints by me as the play clock hits single digits. On the other side of the line of scrimmage, a defender mirrors his movement, which indicates to me that the defense is likely playing man-to-man coverage. This should leave Paul, who is now the only receiver to the right, one-on-one to try to beat the cornerback. A big part of being a good quarterback entails reading the defense before the snap.

The crowd is too loud for a verbal command to snap the ball. I lift my right leg slightly, letting the center, who is looking between his legs, know I am ready. He counts, *Thousand one, thousand two*; then he fires the ball seven yards into my outstretched hands.

The play explodes with sounds of colliding football pads. I look to the center of the field first merely to keep the safety from drifting right, giving the play an opportunity to develop.

I feel a threat close by to my left, my blindside. The defensive end has gotten a great jump on the tackle and is closing quickly. I step up in the pocket, just as a hand grazes the back of my jersey. I feel the pressure of fingers scraping along my back. Very close to a sack. *Too close.*

To maintain their blocks, the offensive line has followed the pass rush and split to the right and left, leaving a large opening in the middle of the field. I take advantage and step forward a few yards, buying a little extra time. For a moment I consider trying to run, but a linebacker floating in the middle of the field, a spy, eliminates that option.

I snap my head to the right, getting back to my original target. Paul has run an out-and-up pattern, beating the coverage by about a yard. It's a small window, but I'm going for it. I settle my feet, pull the ball up behind my head, and let it rip as hard as I can throw it. The pass is a laser.

Paul leaps in the air in the end zone, extending his hands to make the catch. The cornerback reaches with his left hand to deflect the incoming pass, but the ball is in the exact location I want it, just a few inches beyond the defender's hand. Paul snatches the ball in the air, like the talons of a hawk grabbing its prey. As he comes down on the edge of the end zone, he tries to keep his toes in bounds while the defender pushes him, sending him tumbling several yards. No question he caught the ball, but were his feet in bounds?

A side judge trailing the scene steps into view and swings his arms back and forth. *Incomplete? No!*

Another referee comes running in to discuss the matter. I see some heads nod and then a repeat of the "incomplete pass" signal. My heart sinks. That was my best throw of the game. It was the kind of pass I never could have made when I first started playing football. Many years ago, at my first quarterback tryout, I was embarrassed by my ineptitude. I was terrible. My passes were noticeably weaker than the other two quarterbacks competing for the starting job. They had zip on the ball, and my passes fluttered like a sick bird. I became the third string quarterback by default. After that first season, I considered switching positions or quitting altogether; but I hate giving up.

The following spring, I set up a target to throw at. I nailed together two two-by-fours in the shape of a "t" and buried the bottom in the ground. For the next three months, I spent virtually every day throwing as hard as I could at the target. I rested only when I thought I might injure my arm, but that was rare.

I gave myself two points for hitting the middle of the target and one point for hitting either side of the horizontal bar, which symbolized the hands of my would-be receiver. My rule was that every day I had to exceed the score of the prior day.

By the end of the summer, I was outside for hours, trying to hit the quota. My arm was shredded from all the work; but when it fully recovered, I was a different quarterback. I could really fire the ball with accuracy. Coach was shocked at the difference in my passes that following year. I earned the starting job and never gave it back.

Now, after my incompletion to Paul, I begin jogging slowly off the field. Dejected. Then the crowd, which went silent, starts to murmur. I notice the buzz getting louder as more people take notice of the replay on the big screen. It shows Paul's feet come down very close, possibly dragging both feet in the end zone before being pushed out of bounds. For obvious reasons, Coach has decided to challenge the official's call. Is it a touchdown or not?

The play goes under review. The referee examines a variety of camera angles. I have knots in my stomach; the wait is almost unbearable. What is actually five minutes seems like twenty. I may be biased, but it clearly looks like a touchdown to me. How could the side judge have missed that? It can be embarrassing for a referee to reverse a mistake, but it's obviously more important to get the call correct.

The referee finally returns to the field. As he is discussing the play, I can tell he is ruling in our favor. He reverses the call and raises both hands for a touchdown. Fist pumps and high fives erupt on our sideline. I am too overtaken by emotion to join the celebration. It is like reaching the top of a mountain. Did we really just take the lead? I notice myself exhaling, wondering how long I had been holding my breath.

I feel plenty of smacks on my helmet for a job well done, but I know the game isn't over.

Thank goodness that replay exists with all the different camera angles; otherwise the truth would have been missed.

How Does a Replay in Football Relate to Evidence for the Bible?

In sports, a replay shows multiple camera angles to review a play. It provides an opportunity to confirm what truly happened. It enables referees to correct a potential mistake, even if it's an embarrassing error. Replay is about getting things right in sports.

A somewhat similar principle applies to the reliability of the Bible. We don't have the original books from the Bible, but we can be confident that the Bible we have today has the original content. How is that? Based on reviewing and comparing multiple copies (manuscripts) of the New Testament, we can confirm the original content.[68] Moreover, we can be confident that the authors told the truth, because the Bible includes embarrassing details in the accounts.

Let's look at both points in a little more detail.

Since We Don't Have Original Documents, How Do We Know the Bible We Have Today Is What the Authors Wrote?

There are literally thousands of manuscripts (copies) of the New Testament (NT).[69] This fact allows historians to crosscheck all the various copies, in case there are slight variations or errors from copying by hand, to confirm the content of the original writing. Similar to reviewing a variety of camera angles to get the right call in sports, historians can review thousands of NT copies to confirm the original content. There is no other ancient document that has nearly this many manuscripts.[70] It has been estimated that the New Testament we have today was copied with over 99 percent accuracy, which is very strong, particularly for an ancient document.[71]

The Old Testament also has significant manuscript support, including the Dead Sea Scrolls.

Even if We Are Confident We Have the Original Content, How Do We Know the Authors Told the Truth?

The Bible includes embarrassing details, which the authors wouldn't have included if they were fabricating a lie. It may be embarrassing for a referee to overturn a blatant mistake, so when he or she does so, we can trust it's the truth. Similarly, when a NT author includes an embarrassing detail in the account, it's more likely that the account is the truth. This principle of embarrassment is one tool historians use to evaluate the credibility of an account in literature.[72] A biblical author wouldn't include something in the account that may portray himself or his religion in a negative manner unless it were true.

What Are Some Examples of Embarrassing Details in the Bible?

There are numerous examples of embarrassing details throughout the Bible (Old Testament and New Testament). Adam and Eve rebelled against God and tried to pass the blame. Noah got drunk. Abraham lied twice about his wife. Moses killed a man. David committed adultery and had the husband killed. The apostle Paul persecuted the Christian church before being converted to a follower of Jesus. These are just a few of many examples of embarrassment. The fact that the Bible doesn't hide them provides good reason to believe the authors wrote the truth.

What about Jesus? Are there embarrassing details that confirm the accounts of Jesus? Absolutely. Let me offer just two.

There are numerous accounts of Jesus performing miracles. In one example, He heals two demon-possessed men, sending the demons into a herd of pigs, which run down a steep bank into the sea and die. When the town comes out to see what has happened, rather than celebrate the miracle or show reverence to Jesus, they ask Him to leave the region. Below is the reaction of the men watching over the pigs as well as the people of the town. "Then the men who tended them fled. They went into the city and reported everything— especially what had happened to those who were demon-possessed. At that, the whole town went out to meet Jesus. When they saw Him, they begged Him to leave their region" (Matthew 8:33–34 HCSB).

If the author was fabricating a lie, the reaction from the town wouldn't have been fear but rather adoration or worship.

Another example is when Jesus predicted His death and Peter tried to rebuke Him. In response, Jesus rebuked Peter, calling him "Satan." "Then Peter took Him aside and began to rebuke Him, 'Oh no, Lord! This will never happen to You!' But He turned and told Peter, 'Get behind Me, Satan! You are an offense to Me because you're not thinking about God's concerns, but man's'" (Matthew 16:22–23 HCSB).

Since Peter became a leader of the church, this embarrassing detail supports the truth of the Gospels and this specific event when Jesus predicted His death. If the early church were fabricating these writings, they wouldn't have included this embarrassing detail about a church leader.

Overall, embarrassing details provide powerful evidence that the accounts in the Bible aren't fabrications. The authors recorded the truth.

Skeptic: I Don't Believe the Bible Because It's Filled with Miracles and Ridiculous Supernatural Events (Such as Talking Snakes)

Doesn't the beginning of the universe already prove a miracle occurred? There is evidence for other miracles, but this one event (creation of something from nothing) should dismiss the notion that miracles are impossible. When compared to the creation event, every other miracle in the Bible (for example, walking on water, healings, and so forth) is rather easy to believe.[73]

Moreover, if we have any other good reasons to believe God exists, then miracles must be possible.[74] We have already seen significant evidence for God, so miracles in the Bible aren't difficult to believe.

Summary Point: Based on thousands of manuscripts (including early copies), we can be confident that the Bible we read today hasn't changed but is the original writing; and based on numerous embarrassing details, we can be confident the accounts are true.

The next time you see a replay in football with multiple camera angles and watch a referee overturn a call based on the truth (such as the touchdown in this story), perhaps it will remind you that there are multiple manuscripts and embarrassing details that support the reliability and truth of the Bible.

10
Predictions

Score:

Chad's team: 24
Adam's team: 28

Time remaining:

Fourth quarter, twelve minutes left in the game

The ball is sitting on the ground at midfield. Both teams huddle, scheming for the next play. We've got possession with a chance to build on our lead. Scoring another touchdown would give us a double-digit advantage, putting a lot of pressure on Chad.

I bring the offense to the line; both sides settle into their formations. I pause for a moment as I recognize this look from the defense; I have seen it in film study.

They are disguising a blitz from the left—I know it.

I bark out final assignments and point to a couple defenders who are of particular concern. I line up directly behind the center so the defense has to guard against a handoff. We want them to respect the run, but that's not the plan. I give one final look to the left and right for any last-second movement by the defense.

Nothing. Let's go.

I yell, "Ready...Set...Go!"

I receive the ball and drop back, taking about five steps. The play is designed with three parts—one and two setting up three. First, I pump a fake throw to the right at a receiver streaking down the sideline to move the safety back. Next, I look to my right, where the running back is headed, forcing the linebacker on that side of the field to follow him. Both actions create a nice opening for my tight end, who has released from the right side of the line. Everything is unfolding exactly as designed. Good thing because the offensive line is breaking down.

I see the hand of a defensive lineman go up in front of me, who is anticipating a pass. It blocks my vision slightly, but I have no issue getting off the pass. This could be a nice gain. I let it rip.

Just as the ball is leaving my hand, I see the linebacker from the opposite side of the formation flashing across the field from the left. There is no way he could have reacted that fast and covered that much ground. He must have been anticipating the route. A voice inside my head screams, *No!*

Since the pass is thrown in a straight line instead of an arc, the linebacker easily steps in front of the flight path. He raises his hands and easily snatches the ball in the air. I have already started running toward the play, anticipating the inevitable; but someone else tackles him before I get there.

I leave the field and slam my helmet to the ground. My anger consumes me. A teammate tries to console me. I ignore him and walk away. I don't want to be comforted right now. I am furious. Livid. Filled with rage.

My anger has consumed and driven me most of my life, but I haven't reached this level since a year ago when my dad and I had our final words. He was giving me one of those told-you-so speeches that I was absolutely not in the mood for. Our voices escalated quickly.

"I don't care if you're my father. You don't own me! I'm the master of my own life!" I said with ferocity.

My father responded at a lower level but with sternness, "You are the master of your *decisions*, but not your *destination*. Your choices have consequences, some beyond your control."

We exchanged a few more verbal shots before I gave a dismissive wave and headed for the door. Before it slammed behind me, I delivered one final remark. "I hate you."

Right now I sense that someone hates me. I see Coach Stan glaring at me. No doubt he is furious about my interception. He doesn't say anything. The look is enough.

I thought I was filled with anger, but his rage is downright scary.

Nobody else says anything to me on the sideline, good or bad. I stare at the field as Chad's team takes over possession of the football. I shake my head in disgust. I can't believe they anticipated that play. My confidence has turned to concern. Have I just blown my chance? Will I regret that one pass for the rest of my life?

Accurate predictions come from intelligence.

What Aspect of Football Relates to Evidence That God Inspired the Writing of the Bible?

Football coaches and players try to predict what the opposing team will do. They study the tendencies of players and coaches. How does each player move and react? What decisions do certain coaches make in specific situations? Based on this analysis, teams make educated guesses about the future. Sometimes they're right; sometimes they're wrong.

What if a coach could predict the future with 100 percent accuracy *all* the time? You would consider that coach not only a reliable authority but also divine—godlike. Obviously that isn't possible in football, but it is with the Bible.

The Bible contains hundreds of predictions about the future ("prophecies"). Unlike football, it's never wrong; it's 100 percent accurate. How is this possible? The predictions aren't educated guesses, because the Bible wasn't written by man alone.

The Bible claims to be inspired by God—not that God necessarily dictated word for word, but He guided each author to write specific content within his respective writing style.[75] Below are just two Bible verses that claim divine inspiration:

- "*All Scripture is inspired by God* and is profitable for teaching, for rebuking, for correcting, for training in righteousness" (2 Timothy 3:16 HCSB, emphasis added).

- "First of all, you should know this: no prophecy of Scripture comes from one's own interpretation, because no prophecy ever came by the will of man; instead, *moved by the Holy Spirit, men spoke from God*" (2 Peter 1:20–21 HCSB, emphasis added).

Divine inspiration is a bold claim, but if true, then our perspective in reading and following the Bible should change radically. It isn't simply another book. Rather than reading it out of obligation or guilt, it should be our desire to learn from and respond to God's Word.

What Are Some Reasons to Believe God Inspired the Bible?

First is Jesus. He is a reliable authority (more on that later), and He spoke as though the Bible came from God. Jesus referred to the Old Testament as a source of truth when countering temptations from Satan (for example, Matthew 4:1–11) as well as in His responses to Jewish leaders who opposed Him (for example, Mark 12:24–27).

More directly, Jesus stated that when David wrote Psalm 110, the Holy Spirit guided him. "*David himself says by the Holy Spirit*: The Lord declared to my Lord, 'Sit at My right hand until I put Your enemies under Your feet'" (Mark 12:36 HCSB, emphasis added).

These points relate to Jesus's reference to the Old Testament. Regarding the New Testament, Jesus prophesied that the Holy Spirit would guide His disciples when He was gone; this included guiding some of them who wrote the New Testament.[76] "I have spoken these things to you while I remain with you. But the Counselor, the Holy Spirit—the Father will send Him in My name—will *teach you all things and remind you of everything I have told you*" (John 14:25–26 HCSB, emphasis added).

The second reason supporting divine inspiration is the *gradual disclosure of one plan* over many centuries through many different authors. All sixty-six books of the Bible are written by at least forty different authors over a period of about fifteen hundred years, but they fit together and provide one unifying story—God's salvation for mankind.[77]

The Old Testament discloses the condition of mankind (rebellion and broken relationship with God) and the need for a Savior (sacrifice required for sin); and in the New Testament, Jesus, the Messiah, physically arrives, and His death provides a means of salvation. How is it possible for one primary message (God's salvation plan for mankind) to be revealed gradually over hundreds of years through so many different authors? A divine source (God) guiding the entire process of the content and assembly of the Bible is the best explanation.

The third reason for divine inspiration is prophecy. The Bible makes many specific predictions about the future that have been fulfilled. Some people try to predict the future, but only God does so with 100 percent accuracy.[78] In the book of Isaiah, God makes it clear that only He can truly predict the future.[79] "Remember the former things, those of long ago; I am God, and there is no other; *I am God, and there is none like me. I make known the end from the beginning*, from ancient times, what is still to come. I say, 'My purpose will stand, and I will do all that I please'" (Isaiah 46:9–10 NIV, emphasis added).

How Many Prophecies Are in the Bible?

There are hundreds of predictions in the Bible. According to author J. Barton Payne, there are 1,817 predictions (1,239 in the

Old Testament and 578 in the New Testament).[80] Many have been fulfilled, while some haven't occurred since they pertain to the end of the world. According to author John F. Walvoord, about half of the prophecies in the Bible have been fulfilled in a literal manner.[81] That is far too many to be a coincidence, providing further proof that God directed the content of the Bible.

How Many Prophecies Are There about the Messiah, and Do They Align with Jesus?

One category of prophecies is about the Messiah, the person who would provide a way of salvation from eternal punishment. The Old Testament, which was written hundreds of years before Jesus was born, contains these predictions. According to Christian apologist Josh McDowell, there are sixty *major* messianic prophecies[82]; and, according to J. Barton Payne's *Encyclopedia of Biblical Prophecies*, there are 191 total messianic prophecies.[83] *The mathematical chance of one person fulfilling all of them is virtually impossible,*[84] *yet Jesus did.* This is a powerful testimony proving His identify as Messiah as well as God's inspiration of the Bible.

Let's look at just a few examples of messianic prophecies:

Birthplace

In the book Micah, there is a prophecy about the birthplace of the Messiah being in Bethlehem (verse below), which Jesus fulfilled (as recorded in the Gospel of Luke 2:4–7). "*Bethlehem* Ephrathah, you are small among the clans of Judah; One will come from you to be ruler over Israel for Me. *His origin is from antiquity, from eternity*" (Micah 5:2 HCSB, emphasis added). In this verse, the reference to One whose origin is from eternity is akin to God.

Lineage

There are multiple points in the Old Testament that predict the genealogy of the Messiah, which is confirmed in detail in the New Testament (Matthew 1:1–16 and Luke 3:23–38). Below is one example of an OT genealogy prophecy, where God told Abraham that everyone on earth would be blessed through his lineage; blessing all people on earth, not just the Israelites, was accomplished through Jesus. "I will bless those who bless you, I will curse those who treat you with contempt, and *all the peoples on earth will be blessed through you*" (Genesis 12:3 HCSB, emphasis added).

Miracles

There are some predictions about what the Messiah would do, such as performing miracles.[85] As recorded in the Gospel of Matthew (11:2–5), when John the Baptist sought confirmation that Jesus was the Messiah, Jesus referred to a prophecy from Isaiah, which pertained to healings Jesus was performing. "Say to the fainthearted: 'Be strong; do not fear! Here is your God; vengeance is coming. God's retribution is coming; He will save you.' Then the eyes of the blind will be opened, and the ears of the deaf unstopped. Then the lame will leap like a deer, and the tongue of the mute will sing for joy, for water will gush in the wilderness, and streams in the desert" (Isaiah 35:4–6 HCSB).

Salvation

The Old Testament predicts that the Messiah would die for mankind, which is clearly the focus of the New Testament. In the Old Testament, Isaiah 53 refers to a suffering servant, and it is one of the most powerful prophecies about the Messiah. Below is just one verse from this powerful prophecy, which is strikingly comparable to Jesus. "But He was pierced because of our transgressions, crushed because of our iniquities; punishment for our peace was on Him, and we are healed by His wounds" (Isaiah 53:5 HCSB).

There are numerous other OT prophecies regarding the Messiah that are fulfilled in Jesus, but hopefully the references above provide a few helpful examples. For more details, I would recommend Ralph O. Muncaster's book *Examine the Evidence* (2004) (particularly pp. 325–361).

What Is Typology?

Typology is when a person, event, or thing recorded in the Old Testament foreshadows Jesus in the New Testament.[86] It is an *indirect prophecy* from the Old Testament about who the Messiah would be or what He would do. There are several interesting, powerful examples of men from the Old Testament that parallel Jesus's ministry (including Adam, Noah, Abraham, Joseph, Moses, David, Elijah, and Elisha).[87] These striking similarities provide additional support that Jesus was the Messiah and that God inspired the Bible.

One example of an event that is a typology is found in Genesis 22. At God's request, Abraham was willing to sacrifice his son, Isaac (God stopped Abraham since He detests child sacrifice); but this event clearly foreshadowed God's salvation plan to send His Son (Jesus) to actually die for mankind.[88]

In another OT example, Joseph's own brothers rejected him. He was unjustly accused and condemned, and he had a meal with his brothers prior to revealing himself alive (similar events to Jesus).[89]

One of my favorite examples of typology comes from an account in the book of Numbers (Old Testament) – a bronze snake that was hung on a pole to save people foreshadowed Jesus's sacrifice on the cross to save mankind.[90] Let's look at some of the details.

When the Israelites grumbled against God, they were punished with poisonous snakes, which represent sin. God told Moses to hang a snake on a pole, and anyone who looked at the pole would be healed. "The Lord said to Moses, 'Make a snake and put it up on a pole; anyone who is bitten can look at it and live.' So Moses made a bronze snake and put it up on a pole. Then when anyone was bitten by a snake and looked at the bronze snake, they lived" (Numbers 21:8–9 NIV).

There is no way Moses could have known that this event was going to foreshadow Jesus being crucified on a cross. Hundreds of years later, Jesus referred to this event about Himself as the means of salvation. "Just as Moses lifted up the snake in the wilderness, so the Son of Man must be lifted up, that everyone who believes may have eternal life in him" (John 3:14–15 NIV).

The best explanation for this extraordinary foreshadowing of Jesus's crucifixion is that God inspired the Bible.

Skeptic: Isn't It More Likely That the Predictions Are Vague and That Christians Try to Make Them Fit with Actual Events after the Fact?

Even if some prophecies seem vague, there are far too many to dismiss them all as mere coincidence. Moreover, the OT was written well before Jesus was born[91], yet He fulfilled all the messianic prophecies.

Summary Point: Fulfilled prophecies support the contention that God inspired the Bible (it wasn't simply written by man alone) and that Jesus is the Messiah as predicted by the Old Testament.

The next time you see a team make a correct prediction in a game (such as a play call that leads to an interception, similar to the story and picture below), perhaps it will remind you of prophecies in the Bible as evidence that it comes from God.

11

Identity

Score:

Chad's team: 24
Adam's team: 28

Time remaining:

Fourth quarter, two minutes left in the game

I never see him coming. It is the first time in the game that I
have completely missed a blitz. It comes from my blind side. My
eyes are downfield, and I am close to pulling the trigger when I get
crushed from behind. It feels like a cannonball slamming into my
lower back. My head snaps back, wanting to stay where it has been
despite my body thrusting forward. If I were a small tree, the hit
would have cut me in half. There is no way to hold onto the ball.

Now I am in the process of heading to the ground. It feels like
slow motion. The defender has my arms wrapped up so I cannot
brace my fall. The tackler finishes slamming me to the ground. My
left shoulder connects first, absorbing most of the pain. My body
splashes some snow from the ground, spraying my face. Butterflies
eat at my stomach as I am consumed with anxiety, hoping my team
gets the fumble.

I hear someone yell, "Ball!"

I lift my head and see a pile of bodies, hoping desperately that
my team recovers the football. It takes a couple of minutes for the

refs to sort the melee. Finally, the head referee raises a fist, signaling fourth down. Our team has recovered.

Thank goodness. My mistake could have really cost us.

I slowly rise to my feet. It is too painful to stand fully upright. My back is throbbing with pain, reminding me of the way it feels after shoveling heavy snow. Leaning forward, I gingerly walk off the field.

My punt team is lining up. Chad will get the ball back with a chance to take the lead. My defense has played great in the second half, not allowing a single point. I hope it will continue.

A strong punt could pin Chad's team back. Fortunately, we have a great punter who can kick the ball high, allowing our team to get to the ball carrier with little room to return it.

I look downfield and am absolutely stunned to see Chad back there to receive the kick. Their primary punt returner went down with an injury. Chad may be sure handed and fast, but I have never seen a starting quarterback field a punt. Even though this is the final two minutes of the season, he is far too valuable to risk injury. Maybe it's some kind of trick play?

I notice Chad motioning with his finger at each of his teammates on the field, counting to ensure that they have eleven. Knowing Chad, I wouldn't be surprised if he lobbied the coaches to field the punt. He has no fear in pursuing what he wants.

More than once, he has tried to pursue me and restore our relationship. I routinely pushed him away, but it never seemed to stop him. After the major blowup with Dad about a year ago, Chad and I met at the park. It was nostalgic, bringing back memories of when we played football with the neighborhood kids. We sat on the bench, catching up with some small talk, before Chad got to his primary agenda.

"I'm worried about you, Adam." Chad said.

"More than usual?" I responded with sarcasm.

"Yeah, I talked to Dad," Chad continued.

I interrupted before he finished. "There are two sides to every story."

Chad looked at me before proceeding, his eyes showing the care of an older brother. "Your anger concerns us both. I know you think it drives you, but it continues to lead you down a dark path."

Ironically, I felt some anger start to creep in. I hated these conversations. I had my fair share with my girlfriend, Elliana, as well.

Why can't everyone leave me alone?

"If this is how our conversations are going to be, we can stop meeting." My tone was sharp and threatening. I wasn't bluffing.

"Adam," Chad started to respond, but I didn't want to hear it. I have a short fuse, and it was lit. I just knew he wasn't going to stop. I stood up as a sign that our conversation was ending. And so was our relationship.

"You don't need to pursue me anymore Chad," I stated with firmness, staring intently into his eyes. "I don't need you, especially if you are going to tell me how to live my life." I repeated louder and with more intensity, "I don't need you. I don't need anyone!"

I turned and walked away, not waiting for a response. No goodbye. No more words. It didn't end quite as loud or harsh as it had with my dad, but it put up a wall between us; and it is still there. After that day, I continued to sink in anger as well as depression and even broke off my relationship with Elliana.

When I'm not playing football, I feel the reality of being alone. I don't want to admit it, but I miss everyone. I bury my pain with anger, and right now I want to see Chad get smashed on this punt.

The punting team is set up in a traditional formation. There are eight men in the middle to block for the punter and two gunners on the outside, left and right, to attack the ball carrier. Their mission? Drop the punt returner as quickly as possible. This time that is my brother.

The center snaps the football back to the punter. It is a little low, but the punter fields it. He takes two steps, drops the ball, and kicks it dead on with his right leg, which extends straight up in the air. It is a booming kick—very high. I lose track of it and decide to look downfield.

I see Chad take several steps forward and to the right to get in position for the catch. It seems to be taking forever to come down to him, and a couple of players from my team are closing quickly.

Although Chad cannot take his eyes off the ball, he must know his adversaries are approaching. I see him extend his right hand in the air, waving it back and forth. I also hear him yell, "Fair catch. Fair catch. Fair catch."

I let out a small sigh of disappointment. *Fair catch.* No wonder they sent Chad out to field the punt. He was never going to return the ball and risk injury. Just secure the catch. They must not have faith in someone else fielding the punt.

A second later the ball drops into Chad's arms. He makes the catch cleanly but then gets absolutely blasted by one of my gunners, who was running downfield to make the hit. Chad goes flying backward several yards. Somehow he holds on to the ball, but his helmet goes sailing backward. It hits the ground and rolls toward the end zone.

This is one teammate of mine I have never liked—J. D. He has a mean streak that even I think goes too far. Maybe he missed seeing Chad's hand in the air. More likely, he chose to ignore it and take a shot at the starting quarterback.

Yellow flags fly in from every direction along with several whistles blowing the play dead. A pushing match has led to a scuffle on the ground. Chad's teammates didn't like the hit, an obvious penalty. Can't say that I blame them. I would hope my team would come to my defense in similar fashion.

Chad gets to his feet as the ref announces, "That is a fifteen-yard penalty." J. D. is also ejected from the game. Coach Stan doesn't argue and doesn't seem to care. Knowing him, he probably liked the hit.

Chad walks slowly to the sideline. He may not have gotten to return the ball, but he did get his team fifteen yards for the penalty. The question is whether he will be healthy enough for their final chance to score.

By raising his hand and yelling, "Fair catch," Chad was very clear about his intentions.

How Does a Fair Catch in Football Relate to Christianity?

A fair catch is when a player raises his hand during a punt to declare his intentions—"I intend to catch the ball and not run." In fact, the rules don't allow him to run; this protects him from being hit while his eyes are upward, tracking the ball. Contact or interference from the kicking team is a penalty.

How does this fair catch relate to Christianity? Jesus, by His words and actions, figuratively raised His hand, declaring not only His intentions but also His very identity. Jesus claimed to be God. Although He gave profound teachings about ethics and demonstrated compassion for the outcast, Jesus was clear that what people believe about His identity and whether they trust in Him is most important. It determines their eternal destiny. Below are two examples from Jesus regarding this point:

> Therefore I told you that you will die in your sins. For if you do not believe that I am [He], you will die in your sins. (John 8:24 HCSB)

> The one who believes in the Son has eternal life, but the one who refuses to believe in the Son will not see life; instead, the wrath of God remains on him. (John 3:36 HCSB)

When Jesus says, "Believe in," He doesn't mean merely to believe that He is God; rather, to believe in Him is to believe He is God *and* to trust in Him for salvation. There is nothing we can do to earn our place in heaven; rather, we *trust in Jesus* to be the substitute for the punishment we deserve. There is more on this later.

What is an example of Jesus claiming to be God? In the Gospel of John (chapter 8), Jesus claimed to have existed before Abraham, who died hundreds of years earlier. In the same chapter, Jesus also took the title "I Am," which is a title that corresponds to God in the Old Testament. God told Moses that His name is "I Am" (Exodus 3:14). The Jews clearly knew what Jesus was saying since they intended to stone Him because they believed He was committing blasphemy. Below is a portion of the Bible passage. "The Jews replied, 'You aren't 50 years old yet, and You've seen Abraham?' Jesus said to them, 'I assure you: Before Abraham was, I am.' At that, they picked up stones to throw at Him. But Jesus was hidden and went out of the temple complex" (John 8:57–59 HCSB).

Another example of Jesus claiming to be God is when the Jewish high priest questioned Him after His capture. "But Jesus remained silent and gave no answer. Again the high priest asked him, 'Are you the Messiah, the Son of the Blessed One?' 'I am,' said Jesus. 'And you will see the Son of Man sitting at the right hand of the Mighty One and coming on the clouds of heaven.' The high priest tore his clothes. 'Why do we need any more witnesses?' he asked. 'You have heard the blasphemy. What do you think?' They all condemned him as worthy of death" (Mark 14:61–64 NIV).

In His response, Jesus confirmed that He is the Son of God. He also took the title "Son of Man," which is very likely a reference to an Old Testament prophecy in Daniel 7 (see vv. 13–14). Based on the reaction of the high priest, who tore his clothes and accused Jesus of blasphemy, Jesus clearly claimed to be God.

Because of this claim, Jesus cannot merely be a religious teacher. If He isn't God, as He claimed to be, He is either a liar (knows He isn't God) or a lunatic (thinks He is God), not merely a good person.[92]

However, based on His miracles, especially His resurrection, Jesus provided proof for His claim to be God.

What Are Some Examples of Jesus's Actions That Demonstrated His Claim to Be God?[93]

1. **Worship**: Jesus accepted worship, which should be directed only to God. This happened on multiple occasions, including after Jesus walked on water[94] and His appearances after His resurrection.[95] If Jesus weren't God, He would have stopped people from worshipping Him.[96]
2. **Forgiveness**: Jesus forgave sins, which can be done only by God. This happened when Jesus healed a paralytic *and* forgave his sins.[97]
3. **Prayer**: Jesus requested prayer in His name, which should be directed only to God.[98]

Did Jesus's Disciples Believe He Was God?

Absolutely. This wasn't something that developed over time; rather, the early church recognized Jesus as God. Consider written testimonies from key apostles—Peter, John, and Paul.

In the introduction of his second book, Peter identified Jesus as God. "Simeon Peter, a slave and an apostle of Jesus Christ: To those who have obtained a faith of equal privilege with ours through the righteousness of our *God and Savior Jesus Christ*" (2 Peter 1:1 HCSB, emphasis added).

In John's Gospel, he described the "Word" as God and identified the "Word" as Jesus ("became flesh"). "In the beginning was the Word, and the Word was with God, and the *Word was God ... The Word became flesh* and took up residence among us. We observed His glory, the glory as the One and Only Son from the Father, full of grace and truth" (John 1:1, 14 HCSB, emphasis added).

In the same chapter of John's Gospel, he said Jesus created everything that had ever been created; consequently, Jesus cannot be created and must be God. "All things were created through Him, and *apart from Him not one thing was created that has been created*" (John 1:3 HCSB, emphasis added).

In Paul's book to Titus, he identified Jesus as our God and Savior. "While we wait for the blessed hope and the appearing of the glory of our great *God and Savior, Jesus Christ*" (Titus 2:13 HCSB, emphasis added).

Skeptic: Jesus Was Either a Legend or Simply a Good Religious Teacher

It's highly unlikely that Jesus or various parts of His story are a legend. The accounts about Jesus come from His disciples, who were willing to die for those claims. Also, the New Testament includes embarrassing details, which wouldn't have been included in a lie.

Moreover, as already mentioned, Jesus's claim to be God rules out the possibility of Jesus merely being a good teacher. If He lied about His identity, He couldn't be good.

Rather, Jesus provided miraculous evidence that proves His claims.

Summary Point: Based on Jesus's words and actions, He clearly claimed to be God; and direct testimony from His disciples supported this claim.

The next time you see a fair catch, perhaps it will remind you that Jesus, by His actions (and words), claimed to be God.

12
ACE

Score:

Chad's team: 24
Adam's team: 28

Time remaining:

Fourth quarter, one minute left in the game

It's hard to fight the desire to celebrate. We're on the verge of winning. I can almost taste it. Chad's team is down to their last chance—fourth down. The ball is at their thirty-eight-yard line, and they need seventeen yards for a first down. Otherwise, it's game over.

I watch Chad break the huddle and calmly take position, scanning the defense, which is clearly playing a prevent scheme. The chances of Chad making this first down are very small. I begin to feel like we've won. I have finally beaten my brother. But I don't feel the happiness I thought I would. It's strange. I should be ecstatic, but I'm not.

The apparent victory has released my anger; but instead of finding relief and happiness, I feel guilt more than anything. Guilt about how I have treated my brother, my father, Elliana, everyone. Anger has fueled my life for so many years, but I'm starting to regret the path I have chosen. *What's wrong with me?*

My attention snaps back to the field. *The game isn't technically over yet.*

The play clock runs down to one second, and the ball is snapped. I see one of our defenders immediately blitzing from the corner, Chad's blindside. This is a bold move to force Chad to throw the ball quickly before his receivers can get downfield past the first down marker. The offensive line is engaged with three other defenders and doesn't see this attacker. Chad almost misses him as well, but at the last second, he spins to the left, leaving the defender grabbing nothing but air.

At this point the pocket is collapsing, and another defender grabs Chad's jersey, trying to drag him to the ground. It's a clash of wills. Although the defender outweighs Chad by about one hundred pounds, Chad is somehow able to muscle away.

Chad is now running for his life toward the right sideline, which happens to be toward me. A third defender dives at his feet, clipping his right heel. Chad stumbles forward. He looks like he is clearly headed to the ground, but he extends his left hand to the grass, keeping his knees from touching. Somehow, someway, Chad rights himself and keeps running toward the right sideline.

His eyes look downfield. He may have thought of running forward, but a defender who was downfield is now running full speed straight at him, approaching quickly. Another defender is chasing him from behind. The defense is closing in from both sides.

I see Chad slow down and gather his feet, setting up in a throwing position. It is a strong windup, and he hurls the ball as far as I have ever seen him throw it. Right after the release, the oncoming defender slams him from the front, right in the midsection, ribs exposed.

That hit is crushing enough, but what makes it worse is that the other defender who was trailing Chad nails him from behind, essentially sandwiching him. There is no give. Two punishing hits come simultaneously, front and back. Chad, completely exposed, sacrificed his body to make that throw. It is such a devastating hit that I almost forget to watch the end result of the pass.

I look far downfield and see Chad's receiver sprinting toward the end zone, bracketed by two defenders. It's a bold throw, way downfield. Going for it all; a very small chance for success. All three players are within a few yards of each other, sprinting toward the location the ball is descending.

I am absolutely shocked to see the ball descend narrowly between the defenders, right into the receiver's hands. It's an absolutely perfect pass, over sixty yards downfield. It couldn't have been thrown any better. The receiver catches the ball in his hands and immediately dives for the end zone, which is only three yards away. The defenders converge on him and grab the receiver's jersey, attempting to drag him down before he crosses the goal line; but when the receiver falls to the ground the football lands right on the line of the end zone.

Touchdown!

The blood drains from my head. In a matter of seconds, my emotions have gone from excitement to guilt, to shock. I cannot believe what I have just seen. It was beyond extraordinary. This is the kind of play that leaves one speechless, eyes wide and jaw hanging open in disbelief.

Only one word comes to mind ...

Miracle.

How Does a "Miraculous" Play in Sports Relate to Evidence for Jesus?

Sports fans marvel at incredible plays, especially at crucial points in big games. Sometimes the only word that comes to mind is *miracle*. Obviously, it isn't a true miracle. No matter how spectacular a play, it doesn't supersede the laws of nature[99]; but we are in such awe that it's the word we use.

The resurrection of Jesus is an actual miracle. No human being comes back to life after three days unless God is involved to supersede the laws of nature. But why believe it actually occurred? Is there evidence?

Absolutely! The majority of historical scholars who are experts on this topic, even religious skeptics, will grant a few core historical facts; and the best explanation for all three listed below is a miraculous resurrection.[100]

1. **Appearances**: After Jesus died, His disciples had experiences (Christians would say "encounters") they believed was the risen Jesus.
2. **Conversions**: At least two nonbelievers had experiences with the risen Jesus that led to their conversion: Paul, who had been a fervent enemy of Christians; and James, the half brother of Jesus, who had been a skeptic.
3. **Empty Tomb**: The tomb where Jesus was laid after death was found empty.

There is no natural explanation that reasonably fits all three points (more on that below). The best explanation for this historical evidence is that Jesus was resurrected, which isn't a big leap if God exists. As we have already seen, there is compelling evidence for the existence of God, which certainly makes miracles possible.

An easy way to remember these three core facts is by using the acronym "ACE"—the first letters of *Appearances, Conversions,* and *Empty tomb.* An ace in sports is the best player, someone the team is counting on. Jesus proved He is God and someone we can count on.

Why Believe Jesus Really Appeared to the Disciples after His Death?

First, multiple authors in the New Testament (including the writers of the Gospels and 1 Corinthians) wrote about the appearances in the Bible. For example, the Gospel of Luke (chapter 24) records certain appearances by Jesus, including evidence of His physical body (Jesus ate food, and invited the disciples to touch His flesh), not simply a vision. Luke also wrote the book of Acts (early church history), which begins by mentioning that Jesus appeared over forty days, providing proof that He was resurrected. "I wrote the first narrative, Theophilus, about all that Jesus began to do and teach until the day He was taken up, after He had given orders through the Holy Spirit to the apostles whom He had chosen. After He had suffered, *He also presented Himself alive to them by many convincing proofs, appearing to them during 40 days and speaking about the kingdom of God*" (Acts 1:1–3 HCSB, emphasis added).

Another reference to Jesus's appearances comes from Paul's first letter to the Corinthians in chapter 15. "For I passed on to you as most important what I also received: that Christ died for our sins according to the Scriptures, that He was buried, that He was raised on the third day according to the Scriptures, and that He appeared to Cephas, then to the Twelve. Then He appeared to over 500 brothers at one time, most of whom remain to the present, but some have fallen asleep. Then He appeared to James, then to all the apostles" (1 Corinthians 15:3–7 HCSB).

This passage of scripture is considered an early creed in Christianity Paul received (Paul added the appearance Jesus made to him in v. 8); it is dated by most scholars to be within two to eight years after the crucifixion of Jesus.[101] This is much too early for the resurrection appearances to be some legend that developed over time.

You may be thinking, *Even though the Bible claims Jesus appeared after His death, why should I believe it?* First, the testimonies include embarrassing details, which the writers would likely not have included if they had been fabricating a lie; and second, the disciples were willing to die for these claims.

Regarding embarrassing details, I will share just two examples. First, the women were the first to see the risen Jesus, not the male disciples (Matthew 28, Luke 24, John 20). If the disciples had been fabricating a lie, they wouldn't have portrayed themselves in a seemingly negative manner (more on this point later in the chapter).

Another embarrassing detail comes at the end of the Gospel of Matthew. "When they saw Him, they worshiped, but some doubted" (Matthew 28:17 HCSB).

This verse includes three important elements:

1. An appearance by Jesus, which refers to His resurrection
2. Worship of Jesus, which supports His claim to be God
3. And an embarrassing detail, which provides evidence that the account is true

This one verse provides the core doctrine of Christianity: Jesus is God, who died and rose from the dead. The fact that the verse includes "some doubted" indicates it wasn't a lie; the event truly happened.

Another reason to believe the disciples really had experiences of the risen Jesus is that they were willing to die for their claims. It's important to note that they weren't simply willing to die for a belief, as many people in history have done; rather, they were willing to die for events they claimed to have seen.[102] These sufferings are recorded in the Bible and the writings of early church fathers.[103]

In summary, multiple sources record the appearances, and we can believe these accounts because they include embarrassing details; and the disciples were willing to die for their belief that the risen Jesus appeared to them.

Why Believe Paul and James Were Converted Based on Jesus's Appearance?

Paul's original name was Saul. The Bible records in multiple sources his violent persecution of the early Christian church[104] and then an experience with the risen Jesus that led to his conversion.[105]

We can believe his testimony, because the Bible and early church fathers record Paul suffering for his faith.[106]

James is the half brother of Jesus (same mother). According to the Bible, Jesus's brothers were skeptics; they didn't believe in Him.[107] Then Jesus appeared to James,[108] and he became a believer and key member of the church.[109] Josephus, a first-century Jewish historian, recorded James's martyrdom.[110]

Why Believe the Tomb Was Really Empty?

The empty tomb is recorded in all four Gospels of the Bible.[111] We can believe these written accounts for the following three reasons (provided by Christian authors and resurrection scholars Gary Habermas and Mike Licona): "Jerusalem Factor," "Enemy Attestation," and "Testimony of Women," which create the acronym "JET."[112]

First, the fact that Christianity started in the same city (Jerusalem) where Jesus was crucified strongly supports an empty tomb. There is no way Christians could have claimed Jesus was resurrected if His body still lay in the tomb.[113] Their opposition could have simply pointed to the sealed tomb or rolled the stone away.

Second, Jewish leaders who were opposing Christians (enemies) claimed that His disciples had stolen the body.[114] They wouldn't have said this if Jesus were still in the tomb. This claim indirectly confirms the tomb was empty.

Third, women were the first to discover the empty tomb, not the male disciples. At this time in Jewish and Roman cultures, a woman's testimony was considered less credible than a man's,[115] so it's highly unlikely the biblical authors would have fabricated this part of the account. In fact, in Luke's account about the empty tomb,[116] the men thought the women were speaking "nonsense"; again, the writers wouldn't have recorded this embarrassing detail if it hadn't been the truth.

Skeptic: Since Miracles Aren't Possible, There Must Be a Natural Explanation

This objection rejects the resurrection—not because of the evidence but because their philosophy excludes miracles as a possibility. But with our souls at stake, shouldn't we be open to the resurrection as a possibility?

The bottom line is that there is no natural explanation that reasonably fits with the historical evidence. What are some examples of these opposing theories? Although there are several, let's look at just three examples to illustrate why they don't fit.

1. **Jesus didn't die on the cross**[117]: This isn't plausible. One of the most likely causes of death for crucified victims is asphyxiation.[118] To exhale, the person needs to pull up on his or her body, which is nailed to a cross. When the person can no longer do this, he or she suffocates and dies. There is no way to fake death in this position. Moreover, Jesus received a spear in His side to ensure death. Finally, this explanation doesn't account for the disciples' experiences or Paul's conversion.

2. **The disciples stole the body**[119]: Since the disciples were willing to suffer and die for their convictions that Jesus rose from the dead, it isn't plausible that they stole the body. Moreover, this theory doesn't explain why Paul or James became believers, since they wouldn't have been in on this scheme.

3. **The disciples hallucinated**[120]: Given that Jesus appeared to groups of people, hallucinations or visions don't fit. Hallucinations do occur, but multiple people don't see the same vision. Moreover, Paul, who was an enemy, likely wasn't in the frame of mind to have a hallucination; he had a separate experience. Also, James had an experience; and given that he was a skeptic, it is likely he also was not in the

frame of mind to have a hallucination. Finally, this doesn't explain how the tomb would be empty.

Also, I believe that certain aspects of the Biblical record oppose this theory. After the resurrection, Jesus handled food and ate with His disciples.[121] Also, as evidence of His resurrection, Jesus offered to have His disciples touch His body.[122] Finally, in another account, some women who were followers of Jesus held His feet and worshiped Him after the resurrection.[123]

Overall, based on historical facts, the best explanation is that Jesus truly was raised from the dead. Is there a better explanation for *all* these historical facts (ACE) other than the resurrection of Jesus?

Summary Point: There is historical evidence (appearances, conversions, empty tomb) that strongly supports the resurrection of Jesus.

The next time you see an extraordinary play in any sport and think "miracle," perhaps it will remind you of a real miracle, the resurrection of Jesus (which confirms His claim to be God and provides salvation for His followers).

13
Decision

Score:

Chad's team: 30 (it will be 31 after the extra point)
Adam's team: 28

Time remaining:

Fourth quarter, less than one minute left in the game

I am so awestruck by the miraculous pass and touchdown that I almost forget to turn back to Chad. When I do, I see that he has *not* gotten up from the devastating hits. His body lies motionless on the ground. Medical attendees run in from Chad's sideline. One of them is an athletic trainer I recognize. Her name is Mary; she knows our family well. They surround Chad, kneeling next to him. Some players also circle around.

I'm startled by my coach yelling my name, calling me over. No doubt he wants to talk football. What is our plan with so little time left on the clock?

It's not easy to make my way over to Coach. I feel odd, a little disoriented. Hazy. Not physically ill but emotionally numb. I need to consciously focus on walking, forcing my legs to take me over to Coach. He never says a word about Chad; instead he suggests a few plays for our next possession.

I'm not sure how much I even hear Coach. I feel a pull to turn back and make sure my brother is walking off the field. After a couple of minutes, the draw is too strong; I turn my head quickly to see what is happening. My heart sinks when I see medical personnel placing Chad on a cart.

"Adam!" my coach snaps. "We are getting the ball back! Your brother will be fine. Focus on what is at hand!"

Fine? A cart doesn't indicate he will be fine.

I shake my head, trying to discard my emotions. Coach keeps talking football. He pauses from me to direct his words to the microphone on his headset, chatting with the offensive coordinator.

"Adam." I hear a female voice from behind. I turn and see it is Mary, the athletic trainer. "It's really serious. Your brother is in bad shape." The look on her face is panic. The look in her eyes says more than the words. I can tell she felt she needed to share this news.

"Wha ... What do you mean?" I ask, needing more information.

"He may have internal bleeding. I need to go." She turns and runs, not waiting for a response. My knees get weak, and I fight the impulse to vomit.

The next thirty seconds feel like the weight of the world is on my shoulders. I want to finish my dream. This is my opportunity to lead my team to victory. I have spent years working to get to this moment.

But seeing Chad lying on the field, vulnerable and injured, did something inside me. It broke my heart. It shattered the barrier I had put between us. I feel guilt. Remorse. Shame. I am the one who plays with anger, testing ethical boundaries. If anyone deserved to get injured, it should have been me, not him. The anger is gone; what remains is raw guilt. I have this feeling that nothing matters more than my brother. *There is just no way I can finish the game.*

I tell Coach Stan I have to go. The look on his face is that of shock. His eyes burn with disdain and hatred. I don't care. Not waiting for any further reaction from him, I turn to run for where I think the cart is headed.

It takes a couple of minutes, but I track them down. I see a stretcher heading rapidly toward an ambulance and catch up just in time.

"Chad!" The medical personnel pause for a moment. I force my way between a couple of people, seeing Chad is conscious. Barely.

What do you say in those moments when you are worried this could be the last time you see someone? "Chad, I am truly sorry for everything. I love you. Please get better." The look on my face begs him to hang in there and be okay.

Chad doesn't speak but nods, which seems to be all he can muster. It is enough for me. It means he heard me, acknowledging my words. He doesn't have to respond. His love isn't something I ever questioned.

I want to say more, but there is no opportunity. Medical personnel push the stretcher into the ambulance. I try to enter as well but am not allowed. Our encounter seemed longer but was really only a few seconds.

The doors close. The siren turns on, and the ambulance pulls away.

I never saw my brother alive again. On the way to the hospital, he died from internal bleeding.

As I reflect on that day many years later, I have no regrets about my decision to leave the game and reconcile with my brother. None. Our team lost, and many football fanatics expressed their extreme displeasure with my leaving the game. But my team would have lost anyway. The ensuing kickoff was fumbled and lost. A part of me was relieved, because I would likely have carried some guilt for leaving my team.

Nonetheless, I can honestly say that those final moments with my brother changed my life. I turned from my anger, choosing my brother over selfish pride. I reconciled with him before it was too late. It was the most important day of my life because it changed everything for me. I still love football, but I learned that while dreams are important, there are some things, such as family, that are a much higher priority.

I reconnected with Elliana, who was so gracious to have me back. Now many years later, we are happily married with three children. I decided to leave my life of anger and follow a better path. I became a Christian.

And finally, my relationship with my Father was restored.

How Does This Relate to Your Spiritual Journey?

The end of this story was about a decision: finish a personal goal or restore a broken relationship. The former focuses on self; the latter is a selfless act of reconciliation. In the story, they were at odds with each other; only one path was possible.

This decision represents the purpose of life. All of us decide what is most important—our selfish desires or restoring the relationship with our Creator. There is certainly nothing wrong with pursuing passions and dreams in life. That isn't my point. Rather, it is about deciding what comes first: yourself or God. Ironically, you cannot choose both; only one can have ultimate priority. There is a point of tension between following *all* our selfish desires or loving and following God, making ourselves accountable to Him.

Chad sacrificed his body[124] for a miraculous play to win the game; Jesus sacrificed His body for the sins of mankind. Whoever believes in Him is saved. His sacrifice covers our sin—if we accept this gift.

Do we believe God exists and put our trust in Jesus for salvation, leading to the gates of heaven? Or do we choose our desires over God and chase the passions of this world? God won't force anyone to come to Him. This is the purpose of life; everyone decides his or her eternal destination.

14
Symbolism

I hope the football illustrations have been helpful in understanding some of the evidence for God and Christianity.

In addition to these illustrations, the story also includes a second line of symbolism related to Christianity. Each chapter includes events that symbolize key events in the Bible. Although the football story in this book is fiction, the Christian story recorded in the Bible is an actual account of the history of the universe and God's plan of salvation for mankind.

The symbolism discussed below isn't meant to be a perfect match, and there is no substitute for reading the Bible. But hopefully it's helpful in understanding an overview of important events in Christianity.

Let's review key aspects of each chapter and how they align with Christian teaching about the history of the universe:

- **Creation**: In chapter 1, the beginning of the game represents the beginning of the universe. The kickoff symbolizes the event when God (known as "I AM" in the Bible, "Ian" in the story) created the universe and everything in it. In the story, Adam represents all mankind. Chad represents Jesus, who is the *Ch*rist, God who has come in the form of man (*Ad*am). Coach Stan (Satan) tempts Adam, suggesting his passion (football) would solve all his problems. Satan tries to tempt each of us in a variety of ways, including leading us astray with our passions.
- **The Fall of Mankind**: In chapter 2, Evan makes a big mistake by taking his eyes off the football, which represents

Adam and Eve taking their eyes off God and rebelling in disobedience. Both acts lead to negative consequences. Adam and Eve were real people, and their disobedience, called the "original sin," caused a broken relationship between God and mankind. Although people are still capable of doing good, they are now corrupted with a sinful nature and filled with selfish desires (which is what Adam, in this story, referred to as the heart problems that run in the family and he has inherited; Chad has no blemishes with his heart). Our primary focus is now on ourselves, not on our Creator.

- **Moral Depravity of Mankind**: In chapter 3, there is a brutal "cheap shot" hit in the football game. This represents the sin and wickedness that filled the world after mankind's rebellion. It was so bad that God destroyed most living things with a global flood and started over with mankind through Noah and his family. There is evidence for this flood, but it's beyond the scope of this book. Due to our sin, we all face judgment. The Bible tells us the wages of sin is death[125], which is eternal separation from God (hell).

- **Plan for Salvation Begins**: In chapter 4, Chad calls an audible. He looks at the situation and doesn't like where the play is headed, so he decides to change the play. From a Christian perspective, God saw where mankind was headed (judgment) and started a rescue plan.[126] It may not be a true audible because it was part of God's ultimate plan, but if God hadn't interceded with a rescue plan, we would all be without hope, judgment that would result in eternal separation from our Creator (hell).

- **Survival of Israelites**: In chapter 5, Joe returns from an injury when Adam thinks he is done for the game, scoring a much-needed touchdown. In the Bible, Joseph appeared alive to his family when they thought he was gone forever. His jealous brothers sold him, and his father thought he was dead and would never see him again. However, this was allowed as part of God's plan to put Joseph in a position to save the Israelites from famine. The Israelites were God's chosen people for His rescue plan; and despite their sins, He made sure they survived.

- **Demonstration**: In chapter 6, an amazing play opens a path for Moe to score a touchdown. In the Bible, God used Moses to demonstrate His power to the world and free the Israelites from slavery in Egypt. God performed miracles, including parting the Red Sea. It is through these signs and wonders that God demonstrated His power, love, and care for the Israelites. God made it clear that He alone is God, not the false gods of Egypt and Canaan.

- **Punishment**: In chapter 7, Dave defeats a larger opponent, similar to David defeating Goliath, and scores a touchdown; but a penalty negates Dave's play. Committing the infraction has consequences. On a much larger scale, the Israelites broke God's rules and suffered the consequences of judgment. The Old Testament teaches us that God is holy and has moral rules. As God warned, the Israelites were punished, removed from the land God had provided. In time, they repented and looked forward to a deliverer, a Messiah.

- **Incarnation**: The first half of the football game corresponds to the Old Testament (OT) of the Bible. In chapter 8, there is a shift to the New Testament (NT). Halftime is only about fifteen minutes long, but there was about a four-hundred-year gap between the writings of the OT and NT in the Bible.[127] Although Chad has been in the story all along (same as Jesus in history), Adam sees him emerge from the tunnel without his helmet. This picture symbolizes God entering the world as a man in the person of Jesus. This is called the incarnation.

- **Truth**: In chapter 9, replay helps correct an error. It's about getting the call right. It's about truth, something God cares very much about. In fact, Jesus says He came into the world to testify to the truth (John 18:37).[128] Jesus teaches people about ethics and what is most important in life. He corrects the Israelites' misunderstanding of the Old Testament. He also teaches everyone how to go to heaven; believe in Him. "For God loved the world in this way: He gave His One and Only Son, so that everyone who believes in Him will not perish but have eternal life. For God did not send His Son into the world that He might condemn the world, but that the world might be saved through Him. Anyone who believes in Him is not condemned, but anyone who does not believe is already condemned, because he has not believed in the name of the One and Only Son of God" (John 3:16–18 HCSB). As discussed earlier, to believe in Jesus means to put our trust in Him to save us from punishment for our sins.

- **Fulfilled Prophecy Confirms Jesus Is the Messiah**: In chapter 10, the defense correctly predicts Adam's pass and makes an interception. It's a case of understanding the other team's tendencies to predict the future. On a much larger scale, the Bible provides prophecies about the Messiah. Jesus fits all these messianic predictions, proving His identity and that God truly inspired the Bible. In fact, when John the Baptist asked for confirmation that Jesus was the Messiah (Matthew 11:2–5), Jesus quoted an OT prophecy (Isaiah 35:4–6) that pertained to miracles (healings), which He had fulfilled.

- **Jesus Declares His Identity as God**: In chapter 11, the punt returner called a fair catch, declaring his intentions. He was clear about his intentions both in words (yelling, "Fair catch. Fair catch. Fair catch.") and in actions (raising his hand). With regards to Jesus, He was clear about His identity as God, both in His words and in His actions.

- **Jesus's Death and Resurrection**: In chapter 12, Chad sacrifices his body, taking a fatal blow to make an extraordinary play. His act symbolizes Jesus's sacrifice of

His body through His crucifixion for the sins of mankind (unlike Chad, Jesus rose from the dead). The path to heaven is set, making the crucifixion and resurrection the greatest events in the history of the universe.[129]

- **The Purpose of Life**: In chapter 13, Adam needs to make a choice between pursuing his personal desire or restoring his relationship with his brother. It is akin to our decision—choosing our selfish desires or choosing a relationship with our Creator, accepting Jesus as our Lord and Savior. There is nothing wrong with pursing our passions and dreams but not when they run counter to God. In the story, Adam chooses wisely before the game ends. I hope that you will as well.

If you are interested in learning more about the Christian perspective of the history of the world, I highly recommend Greg Koukl's *The Story of Reality*.

There are many other good Christian books as well, but none are a substitute for reading the Bible, God's Word. If you rarely open it, I highly recommend starting with any of the Gospels (Matthew, Mark, Luke, or John), which describe the ministry of Jesus as well as His death and resurrection.

15
Your Destiny

In the introduction, I said there is nothing more important than knowing the truth about God and going to heaven. But your destiny isn't automatic. It comes down to a decision, your decision.

According to the Bible, everyone is a sinner—someone who violates God's moral rules. Deep down, we all know this is true. We aren't perfectly moral people. We all commit sins. Our guilt confirms that we do wrong.

We also know that doing wrong deserves punishment. Even if we do a lot of good things, they don't negate the wrong things we do. God is loving but also holy, righteous, and just. This means there must be punishment for the wrong things we do. If God simply dismissed our sins, He wouldn't be acting with justice. No amount of good deeds nullifies the sins we have committed against a perfectly holy God.

How does God save mankind, whom He loves, while also punishing their sins? God comes in the form of a man (Jesus) and takes the punishment Himself. Jesus allowed Himself to be crucified, sacrificing Himself for the punishment we deserve. This is the gift God has offered us—grace. But we must accept Jesus as our Lord and Savior, as the apostle Paul wrote in the book of Romans. "If you confess with your mouth, 'Jesus is Lord,' and believe in your heart that God raised Him from the dead, you will be saved. With the heart one believes, resulting in righteousness, and with the mouth one confesses, resulting in salvation" (Romans 10:9–10 HCSB).

Three Questions to Heaven

I hope this book has been helpful in providing some of the evidence for Christianity. To summarize this evidence and help you reflect on your spiritual position, I have provided three major questions and several sub questions. I encourage you to reflect on them with an open mind.

1. **Do You Believe God Exists?**
   A. Is it more reasonable that the universe popped into existence from nothing without a cause (atheism) or that something exists beyond the universe that created it (God)? (Chapter 1)
   B. Is it more reasonable that there are an infinite number of universes and that we are extremely lucky that our planet is able to support life (atheism) or that the universe and earth were intricately designed by a divine architect (God)? (Chapter 2)
   C. Is it more reasonable that moral rules are determined by people or societies (atheism) or that the standard for good and evil is objective (actions are right or wrong independent of the opinions of people) and therefore comes from a source that transcends mankind (God)? (Chapter 3)
   D. Is it more reasonable that literally everything in nature is a random collection of atoms and therefore *all* has the same value or worth (atheism) or that there is a hierarchy of value in nature, with humans at the top since we are created in God's image (God)? (Chapter 3)
   E. Is it more reasonable that information in nature (for example, DNA), which is immaterial, can somehow happen randomly (atheism) or that a divine mind with purpose and intent included this information in creation (God)? (Chapter 4)

F. Is it more reasonable that when people report Near Death Experiences, they are simply images in the brain (atheism), or that people have had real out-of-body experiences because they have a soul created by a divine being (God)? (Chapter 5)

G. Is it more reasonable that our thoughts are simply random chemical activities in the brain and our actions are determined by our genetics reacting to the environment around us (atheism) or that we have an immaterial soul that enables us to think, reason, and make freewill choices (God)? (Chapter 6)

H. Is it more reasonable that evil is defined by people's subjective opinions (atheism) or an illusion (some Eastern religions) or that evil is an objective wrong violating a moral standard applicable to all mankind (God)? (Chapter 7)

➢ Note: Personally, I believe God is the best answer for each of these questions, but what is really powerful is that it takes only one. Conversely, for atheism to be true, it would have to explain all these questions. *What is more likely—atheism is the right answer for all, or God is the right answer for at least one?* That is the power of a cumulative case.

2. **Do You Believe Jesus Is God and Was Resurrected from the Dead?**

A. Is it more reasonable that authors of the Bible lied about certain accounts, while also including some embarrassing details (non-Christian) or that the authors recorded the truth and believers were willing to die for their claims (Christian)? (Chapter 9)

B. Is it more reasonable to believe that the prophecies fulfilled in the person of Jesus are an unbelievable coincidence (non-Christian) or that the Bible is divinely inspired and Jesus is the Messiah (Christian)? (Chapter 10)

C. Is it more likely that Jesus' followers lied about His claim to be God (non-Christian) or that Jesus truly claimed to be God, which led to His crucifixion (Christian)? (Chapter 11)

D. Regarding the resurrection, is there a natural explanation (non-Christian) that accounts for Jesus's appearances to His disciples, the conversions of Paul and James, and the empty tomb (ACE)—or it more reasonable that Jesus was truly resurrected (Christian)? (Chapter 12)

3. **Are You Willing to Follow Jesus as Lord and Trust Him as Savior, Accepting God's Grace to Forgive You of Your Sins?**

A. Do you believe you have ever done anything wrong in life?

B. Do you believe doing something wrong deserves punishment?

C. Given that you have done wrong things in life and that they deserve punishment, does the possibility of being in hell for eternity concern you?

D. Will you accept Jesus as your Savior, substituting the punishment you deserve for the price He paid with His crucifixion, and commit to Him as Lord?

If you answered no to questions one, two, or three, I hope you will seek God with your mind and heart. There is too much at stake.

If you answered yes to questions one, two, and three, the Bible says your sins are forgiven. It's important to grow in your relationship with God—reading His Word (Bible), spending time in prayer, and finding a good church to worship God and fellowship with other believers.

No matter where you are in life—whether you are enjoying great happiness, are suffering from a loss, or are somewhere in between—always remember the following:

> God cares about you, and ultimately there is nothing more important than the eternal destination of your soul.

It seems appropriate to finish with the words of Jesus, which identify the two paths before us. "The one who believes in the Son has eternal life, but the one who refuses to believe in the Son will not see life; instead, the wrath of God remains on him" (John 3:36 HCSB).

Everyone dies. What really matters is where we spend eternity.

Notes

Chapter 1

1 Christian apologist William Lane Craig quotes British physicist and author P. C. W. Davies, regarding the point that not only matter and energy, but also space and time had a beginning. P. C. W. Davies, "Spacetime Singularities in Cosmology," in J. T. Fraser (ed.), *The Study of Time III* (New York: Springer Verlag, 1978), 78–79, quoted in William Lane Craig, "The Kalam Cosmological Argument," in William Lane Craig, ed., *Philosophy of Religion: A Reader and Guide* (New Brunswick, NJ: Rutgers University Press, 2002), 102.

2 William Lane Craig makes the point that something coming from nothing is worse than magic, because with magic at least you have a magician and a hat prior to pulling a rabbit out of the hat. William Lane Craig, *On Guard: Defending Your Faith with Reason and Precision* (Colorado Springs, CO: David C. Cook, 2010), 75.

3 William Lane Craig discusses in detail the impossibility of actually traversing the infinite. Craig, "The Kalam Cosmological Argument," *Philosophy of Religion*, 2002, 97–101.

4 Norman L. Geisler and Frank Turek, *I Don't Have Enough Faith to Be an Atheist* (Wheaton, IL: Crossway Books, 2004), 76.

5 Geisler and Turek, *I Don't Have Enough Faith*, 93.

6 Geisler and Turek, *I Don't Have Enough Faith*, 93.

7 Christian philosopher and author J. P. Moreland makes the point that the cause of the universe is best explained by the free act of a person, since the first event is a cause that comes from a state of no space or time. J.P. Moreland, *Scaling the Secular City: A Defense of Christianity* (Grand Rapids, MI: Baker Academic, 1987), 42.

Christian apologists Norman Geisler and Frank Turek also confirm this point that the cause of the universe must be personal, because the first event required a decision to create the universe from nothingness. Geisler and Turek, *I Don't Have Enough Faith*, 93, 197.

8 Geisler and Turek, *I Don't Have Enough Faith*, 93.

9   Dr. William Lane Craig has written extensively on Christian apologetics and is a major advocate for the Kalam cosmological argument, which provides the basis for my summary logical argument. His argument follows:
1. Whatever begins to exist has a cause.
2. The universe began to exist.
3. Therefore, the universe has a cause.

This argument is referenced in multiple sources as well as debates by Dr. Craig, including one of his major books, William Lane Craig, *Reasonable Faith: Christian Truth and Apologetics* (Wheaton, IL: Crossway Books, 1994), 92.
It is also referenced in one of the articles on his website: https://www.reasonablefaith.org/writings/scholarly-writings/the-existence-of-god/in-defense-of-the-kalam-cosmological-argument/.

Chapter 2

10 William Dembski (Ph.D. in mathematics and philosophy) used the phrase "specified complexity" to describe an effect that was both specific and complex. He claimed that an effect that had specified complexity was best explained by intelligence because they imply a choice was made. William A. Dembski, *Intelligent Design: The Bridge Between Science & Theology* (Downers Grove, IL: InterVarsity Press, 1999), 47, 228, 247.

11 According to Dr. William Dembski, things that have specified complexity are designed and design requires intention. Dembski, *Intelligent Design*, 245.

12 Mark Eastman and Chuck Missler referenced Harold Morowitz, a Yale University physicist, who estimated the chance of spontaneous generation of a life coming from nonlife is one chance in $10^{100,000,000,000}$. Harold Morowitz, *Energy Flow in Biology* (New York: Academic Press, 1968), referenced by Mark Eastman and Chuck Missler, *The Creator Beyond Time and Space* (Costa Mesa, CA: The Word for Today, 1996), 61.

13 Dr. William Lane Craig makes the point that the laws of nature are distinct from certain constants in nature that are part of the mathematical calculations for these laws. For example, gravity is a law in nature with a specific value that is calculated with a precise gravitational constant. Craig, *On Guard*, 108.

14   Hugh Ross, *The Creator and the Cosmos: How the Latest Scientific Discoveries Reveal God* (Covina, CA: RTB Press, 2018), 168–169.

15   Ross, *Creator and the Cosmos*, 168-169.

16   Ross, *Creator and the Cosmos*, 233.

17   Ross, *Creator and the Cosmos*, 169.

18   Craig, *On Guard*, 109.

19   Robin Collins, "The Teleological Argument: An Exploration of the Fine-Tuning of the Universe," in William Lane Craig and J. P. Moreland, eds., *The Blackwell Companion to Natural Theology* (Oxford: Blackwell, 2012), referenced by Nancy Pearcey, *Finding Truth: 5 Principles for Unmasking Atheism, Secularlism, and Other God Substitutes* (Colorado Springs, CO: David C Cook, 2015), 25–26.

20   Geisler and Turek, *I Don't Have Enough*, 105.

21   Ross, *Creator and the Cosmos*, 233. Pages 233-241 list sixty of the parameters and a website is referenced regarding the full list.

22   Ross, *Creator and the Cosmos*, 218, (note: 243-266 provides an abbreviated list of 150 parameters).

23   Ross, *Creator and the Cosmos*, 219.

24   This estimate for the maximum number of planets in the universe comes from Hugh Ross's third expanded edition of the following book: Hugh Ross, *The Creator and the Cosmos: How the Latest Scientific Discoveries Reveal God* (Colorado Springs, CO: NavPress, 2001), 198.

Chapter 3

25   C. S. Lewis discussed the difference between laws of nature and moral laws; he referred to the latter as "Human Nature." Human Nature tells people what they ought to do, which they don't always follow. This is different from the laws of nature, which describe what is happening in nature (gravity, for example). C. S. Lewis, *Mere Christianity* (New York: NY: HarperSanFrancisco, 2001), 17.
According to Christian apologist and author Norman Geisler, natural laws cannot account for morality because nature only describes what something *is* (descriptive); whereas, moral laws provide rules how people *ought* to behave (prescriptive). Norman L. Geisler, *Baker Encyclopedia of Christian Apologetics* (Grand Rapids, MI: Baker Academic, 2006), 500.
Norman Geisler and Frank Turek also reference this argument, writing that moral law is a prescription for how people ought to behave, and a

prescription needs a prescriber, which for humankind is best explained as God. Geisler and Turek, *I Don't Have Enough Faith*, 170–171.

26 William Lane Craig defines the difference between moral duties (I am using the word *rule* instead of *duty*) and moral values. Moral duties are obligations to behave in a certain manner, which determine right and wrong behavior. Moral values determine the value of certain actions or worth of people in nature. Craig, *On Guard*, 130.

27 Craig, *On Guard*, 130.

28 Geisler and Turek, *I Don't Have Enough Faith*, 176.

29 Geisler and Turek, *I Don't Have Enough Faith*, 179. This book discusses how the concept of society getting better or worse indicates a moral law.

30 I have heard Greg Koukl, president of STR, make the point that if God doesn't exist, then morality must be "inside" people, therefore making it subjective. But if it is "outside" us, then it is objective, existing independently from us. Below is a podcast from Greg's radio program. Greg Koukl, "Illustrations to Show That Evil Is Evidence for God," STR, June 15, 2018, https://www.str.org/podcasts/illustrations-show-evil-evidence-god#.W6gCpS2ZOCQ.
   Furthermore, Greg Koukl, in his debate with atheist, Michael Shermer, made the point that moral actions themselves are right or wrong and distinct from our feelings. https://www.str.org/articles/greg-koukl-and-michael-shermer-at-the-end-of-the-decade-of-the-new-atheists#.W6gI1C2ZOCQ.

31 Brett Kunkle provides a good explanation of this point. Brett Kunkle, "Why Do We Need God for Morality?" STR, February 19, 2015, https://www.str.org/videos/why-do-we-need-god-for-morality#.W8Hn3y2ZOYU.

32 Kevin Lewis, "Theological Anthropology: Essential Christian Doctrine Syllabus—Summer 2012," Biola University, 1.

33 Lewis, "Theological Anthropology," 1.

34 Lewis, "Theological Anthropology," 1.

Chapter 4

35 Dr. Werner Gitt's book *In the Beginning Was Information* is a great resource for God being the best explanation for information. In particular, Dr. Werner makes the point that information requires a sender because information comes from the will and intention of a sender. Dr. Werner

Gitt, *In the Beginning Was Information: A Scientist Explains the Incredible Design in Nature* (Green Forest, AR: Master Books, 2005), 52-53.

36 Dr. J. C. Sanford, *Genetic Entropy & The Mystery of the Genome* (Lima, NY: Elim, 2005), 2.

37 Christian apologists Norman Geisler and Frank Turek make this point, while citing the data that was admitted by Oxford University professor Richard Dawkins.

Geisler and Turek, *I Don't Have Enough Faith*, 116, references Richard Dawkins, *The Blind Watchmaker* (New York: Norton, 1987), 17–18, 116.

38 Stephen C. Meyer, *Signature in the Cell: DNA and the Evidence for Intelligent Design* (New York: HarperOne, 2009), 12.

Chapter 5

39 Jeffrey Long with Paul Perry, *Evidence of the Afterlife: The Science of Near-Death Experiences* (New York, NY: HarperOne, 2010), 48–49.

40 Michael B. Sabom, *Recollections of Death: A Medical Investigation* (New York, NY: Wallaby Books, 1982), 52.

41 Long with Perry, *Evidence of the Afterlife*, 44.

42 Long with Perry, *Evidence of the Afterlife*, 48–49.

43 Sabom, *Recollections of Death*, 12.

44 J. P. Moreland, "More Evidence for Life After Death," in *The Apologetics Study Bible*, ed. Ted Cabal (Nashville, TN: Holman, 2007), 1598.

45 Long with Perry, *Evidence of the Afterlife*, 47.

46 John Burke, *Imagine Heaven: Near-Death Experiences, God's Promises, and the Exhilarating Future That Awaits You* (Grand Rapids, MI: Baker Books, 2015), 326.

47 Moreland, "More Evidence for Life After Death," *The Apologetics Study Bible*, 1598.

48 Michael Sabom, "The Shadow of Death," article first appeared in *Christian Research Journal* 26, no. 3 (2003), http://www.equip.org/PDF/DD282-2.pdf, 4.

Chapter 6

49 Moreland, *Scaling the Secular City*, 77.

50 Dr. Jason Lisle has written a great book arguing that logic points to God, specifically Christianity. He contends that logic is grounded in God because

the rules are immaterial and unchanging (same as God). They cannot be rules that come from societies or cultures, because then logic could change; nor can they simply come from brain activity because they could be different between people. Dr. Jason Lisle, *The Ultimate Proof of Creation: Resolving the Origins Debate* (Green Forest, AR: Master Books, 2009), 52–53.

51 Bible: Romans 1:18.
52 Geisler and Turek, *I Don't Have Enough Faith*, 31.
    Clay Jones, *Why Does God Allow Evil? Compelling Answers for Life's Toughest Questions* (Eugene OR: Harvest House, 2017), 111–113.
53 Dr. Michael C. Rea provides a great presentation on the topic of "Divine Hiddeness." I heard him use a different illustration related to why God may seemingly remain hidden to allow for free will (police officer in rearview mirror). Dr. Michael C. Rea, "Why Isn't God More Obvious?" (presentation, "Earnestly Contending" Apologetics conference, New Life Church, Smithfield, RI, November 2008), http://www.epsociety.org/store/default.asp?mode=category&did=8&aid =8000063.
54 Geisler and Turek, *I Don't Have Enough Faith*, 31.
    Clay Jones, *Why Does God Allow Evil?*, 111–113.
55 Gary R. Habermas and J. P. Moreland, *Immortality: The Other Side of Death* (Nashville, TN: Thomas Nelson, 1992), 29.
56 Habermas and Moreland, *Immortality*, 81–82, references Wilder Penfield's experiments and includes a quote from Wilder that stimulating the brain would not trigger a patient to believe something or make a decision. Wilder Penfield, *The Mystery of the Mind: A Critical Study of Consciousness and the Human Brain* (Princeton, NJ: Princeton University, 1975), 76–78.

Chapter 7

57 Geisler and Turek, *I Don't Have Enough Faith*, 390.
58 Craig, *On Guard*, 158.
59 Geisler, *Baker Encyclopedia*, 220.
60 Geisler and Turek, *I Don't Have Enough Faith*, 390.
61 J. P. Moreland and William Lane Craig, *Philosophical Foundations for a Christian Worldview* (Downers Grove, IL: IVP Academic, 2003), 544.
62 Jones, *Why Does God Allow Evil?*, 208.
63 Geisler, *Baker Encyclopedia*, 224.
    Geisler and Turek, *I Don't Have Enough Faith*, 400.

Chapter 8

64 Geisler, *Baker Encyclopedia*, 598.

65 Geisler and Turek, *I Don't Have Enough Faith*, 44-46.

66 Based on a fundamental law in logic known as the "law of noncontradiction," it is impossible for claims that contradict to be true at the same time and in the same sense. Example of a contradiction: I am forty-three years old; I am not forty-three years old. This principle of logic can be found in multiple sources, including R. C. Sproul, *The Consequences of Ideas: Understanding the Concepts That Shaped Our World* (Wheaton, IL: Crossway Books, 2000), 41–42.

67 Geisler, *Baker Encyclopedia*, 742.

Chapter 9

68 Geisler and Turek, *I Don't Have Enough Faith*, 228.

69 There are 5,686 partial and complete manuscripts of the New Testament written in Greek between the second and fifteenth centuries as well as thousands of manuscripts in other languages. This fact is cited in Geisler, *Baker Encyclopedia*, 532.

70 Geisler and Turek, *I Don't Have Enough Faith*, 225–226.

71 According to New Testament scholar Bruce Metzger, the New Testament was copied with 99.5 percent accuracy. This was referenced by Geisler, *Baker Encyclopedia*, 532–533.

72 Gary R. Habermas and Michael R. Licona, *The Case for the Resurrection of Jesus* (Grand Rapids, MI: Kregel, 2004), 36, 38–39.

73 Geisler and Turek, *I Don't Have Enough Faith*, 203.

74 Geisler, *Baker Encyclopedia*, 450.

Chapter 10

75 Geisler, *Baker Encyclopedia*, 91-92.

76 Geisler and Turek, *I Don't Have Enough Faith*, 364.

77 A good summary of this point is made by Josh McDowell, *The New Evidence that Demands a Verdict* (Nashville, TN: Thomas Nelson, 1999), 4–7.

78 Ralph O. Muncaster, *Examine the Evidence: Exploring the Case for Christianity* (Eugene, OR: Harvest House, 2004), 286.

79 Muncaster, *Examine the Evidence*, 286.

80 J. Barton Payne, *Encyclopedia of Biblical Prophecies* (London: Hodder & Stoughton, 1973), 674–675, referenced by Geisler, *Baker Encyclopedia*, 609.

81 John F. Walvoord, *Every Prophecy of the Bible: Clear Explanations for Uncertain Times by One of Today's Premier Prophecy Scholars* (Colorado Springs, CO: Chariot Victor, 1999), 10.

82 Josh McDowell, *More Than a Carpenter* (Carol Stream, IL: Living Books, 2005), 98.

83 J. Barton Payne, *Encyclopedia of Biblical Prophecies* (London: Hodder & Stoughton, 1973), 665–670, referenced by Geisler, *Baker Encyclopedia*, 610.

84 Author Ralph Muncaster selected thirty specific prophecies and assigned a probability of one person fulfilling each one by chance. He then calculated the probability of one person fulfilling all of them, which was one chance in 10^{110}. Muncaster, *Examine the Evidence*, 353–355.

85 Muncaster, *Examine the Evidence*, 339–340.

86 *Rose Book of Bible Charts*, vol. 2 (Torrance, CA: Rose Publishing, 2008), 76.

87 *Rose Book of Bible Charts*, 76–82.

88 *Rose Book of Bible Charts*, 78.

89 *Rose Book of Bible Charts*, 79.

90 Ralph O. Muncaster, *Does the Bible Predict the Future?* (Eugene, OR: Harvest House, 2000), 38.

91 Muncaster, *Examine the Evidence*, 327-330.

Chapter 11

92 These three potential options of Lord, liar, or lunatic (not merely a good moral teacher) are based on comments by C. S. Lewis, *Mere Christianity*, 52.

93 Chapter 13 of *I Don't Have Enough Faith to Be an Atheist* provides some great examples of Jesus's claims about His identity, including His actions that indicate His claim to be God (specifically for the latter, see the following source). Geisler and Turek, *I Don't Have Enough Faith*, 344–345.

94 Bible: Matthew 14:33.

95 Bible: Matthew 28:9, 17.

96 In Luke 4:8, Jesus countered Satan's request for worship, saying only God is to be worshipped.

97 Bible: Mark 2:5–7; Luke 5:20–21; 7:48–50.

98 Bible: John 14:13–14.

Chapter 12

99 Christian apologist and author, Norman Geisler defined a miracle as an effect caused by God that interrupts the natural manner or way in which the world operates. Geisler, *Baker Encyclopedia*, 450.

100 The key points are based on Christian historical scholars and authors Gary Habermas and Mike Licona's 4+1 minimal facts approach regarding evidence for the resurrection of Jesus. They are based on historical data that is well evidenced and agreed on by the majority of scholars on this topic (even skeptics). The 4+1 includes the following:
   1. Jesus died by crucifixion.
   2. Jesus's disciples believed that He appeared to them.
   3. Conversion of Paul, who was an enemy of Christians until he experienced the risen Christ.
   4. Conversion of James, who was Jesus's brother and a skeptic until he saw Jesus risen from the dead.
   5. Jesus's tomb was found empty.
   Habermas and Licona, *The Case for the Resurrection of Jesus*, 47, 75.

101 Gary R. Habermas, *The Risen Jesus & Future Hope* (Lanham, MD: Rowman & Littlefield, 2003), 17.

102 Norman Geisler and Frank Turek point out a key difference between the New Testament (NT) Christian martyrs and other martyrs dying for a cause. They may all have sincerity, but NT Christian martyrs also had evidence, having experienced the risen Jesus.
   Geisler and Turek, *I Don't Have Enough Faith*, 294.

103 Some examples from the Bible: Acts 7:54–8:3; Acts 12:1–5; Acts 21:30–36; Acts 14:19; 2 Corinthians 11:24–27.
   There are multiple recordings by early church fathers that support the fact that the apostles were willing to suffer and die for their convictions. Below are examples:
   • First Clement 5:2–7—Habermas and Licona, *The Case for the Resurrection of Jesus*, 57.
   • Polycarp 9:1–2—http://www.earlychristianwritings.com/text/polycarp-lightfoot.html.

- Ignatius of Antioch—Gary R. Habermas, *The Historical Jesus: Ancient Evidence for the Life of Christ* (Joplin, MO: College Press, 1996), 231–232.
- Tertullian— Habermas and Licona, *The Case for the Resurrection of Jesus*, 58.

104 Bible: Acts 8:3; 26:9–11; Galatians 1:13, 23.

105 Bible: Acts 9:1–9; 22:6–21; 26:12–18.

106 Bible: Acts 14:19; 2 Corinthians 11:24–27. Also, early church fathers, including 1 Clement 5:2–7 and Polycarp 9:1–2 (sources identified in previous footnote from this chapter).

107 Bible: Mark 3:20-21; John 7:2–5.

108 Bible: 1 Corinthians 15:7.

109 Bible: Galatians 1:19 (Paul sees James in Jerusalem).

110 Cited in Josephus's work *Antiquities of the Jews 20*, as referenced in Michael R. Licona, *The Resurrection of Jesus: A New Historiographical Approach* (Downers Grove, IL: IVP Academic, 2010), 236.

111 Bible: Matthew 28:1–6; Mark 16:1–6; Luke 24:1–3; John 20:1–8.

112 These three reasons are cited by Habermas and Licona, *The Case for the Resurrection of Jesus*, 70–74.

113 Note: I am using the terms 'Christians' for ease of understanding, but according to the Bible, believers in Jesus were not called Christians until the church in Antioch. "Then he went to Tarsus to search for Saul, and when he found him he brought him to Antioch. For a whole year they met with the church and taught large numbers. *The disciples were first called Christians at Antioch"* (Acts 11:25-26 HCSB, emphasis added).

114 Bible: Matthew 28:11–15.

115 Habermas and Licona, *The Case for the Resurrection of Jesus*, 72.

116 Bible: Luke 24:9–11.

117 Dr. Habermas and Dr. Licona provide a more complete response to this hypothesis, which includes points provided in my summary. Habermas and Licona, *The Case for the Resurrection of Jesus*, 99–103.

118 This comes from an article written in the *Journal of the American Medical Association*, which used modern medical insight to confirm the death of Jesus.
William D. Edwards, Wesley J. Gabel, and Floyd E. Hosmer, "On the Physical Death of Jesus Christ," *Journal of the American Medical Association* 255, no. 11 (March 21, 1986):1461.

119 Dr. Habermas and Dr. Licona provide a more complete response to this hypothesis, which includes points provided in my summary. Habermas and Licona, *The Case for the Resurrection of Jesus*, 93–97.

120 Dr. Habermas and Dr. Licona provide a more complete response to this hypothesis, which includes points provided in my summary. Habermas and Licona, *The Case for the Resurrection of Jesus*, 105–109.

121 Bible: Luke 24:30; Luke 24:41–43; John 21:12–13.

122 Bible: Luke 24:36–40; John 20:24–29.

123 Bible: Matthew 28:9.

Chapter 13

124 The violence of football: My story included some brutal hits and the death of one of the main characters. These elements were needed to add drama and make certain illustrations. They weren't intended to disparage the sport in any way. Football is an aggressive, violent sport; but it also has positive benefits, such as teamwork, discipline, exercise, and entertainment. I hope there continues to be progress made to make the game as safe as possible.

Chapter 14

125 Bible: Romans 6:23.

126 Gregory Koukl, *The Story of Reality: How The World Began, How It Ends, and Everything Important That Happens In Between* (Grand Rapids, MI: Zondervan. 2017), 38.

127 George Knight and James Edwards, eds., *Compact Bible Handbook* (Nashville, TN: Thomas Nelson, 2004), 205.

128 Del Tackett makes this point in a great video series that he teaches, *The Truth Project* (Colorado Springs, CO: Focus on the Family, 2006), DVD.

129 Christian apologist Josh McDowell says that after more than 700 hours of investigation, he believes that the resurrection is either a wicked hoax or the most fantastic fact of history.
Josh McDowell, *The New Evidence that Demands a Verdict*, 203.

Printed in the United States
By Bookmasters